Know
My
Name

Know My Name

A Gay Liberation Theology

RICHARD CLEAVER

Westminster John Knox Press
Louisville, Kentucky

For Mike

Book and cover design by Drew Stevens

First edition

Published by Westminster John Knox Press
Louisville, Kentucky

This book is printed on acid-free paper that meets the American National Standards Institute Z39.48 standard. ♾

PRINTED IN THE UNITED STATES OF AMERICA

96 97 98 99 00 01 02 03 04 — 10 9 8 7 6 5 4 3 2

Library of Congress Cataloging-in-Publication Data

Cleaver, Richard.
    Know my name : a gay liberation theology / Richard Cleaver.
       p.   cm.
    Includes bibliographical references.
    ISBN 0-664-25576-0 (alk. paper)
    1. Homosexuality—Religious aspects—Christianity.   2. Liberation theology.   I. Title.
BR115.H6C6   1995
261.8'35766—dc20   94-34207

Contents

Preface

First, a confession of where I stand in relation to society: I am male and white and from the class we used to call "intelligentsia" (social critic Barbara Ehrenreich has rightly called this term "unduly flattering").[1] This combination of characteristics places me at a specific distance from the center and margins of power in our society, different from where many other gay men and all lesbians stand.

It is not customary for theologians to begin this way. Theology, we claim, is "the Queen of Sciences," pure and above the entanglements of the world, inhabiting a divine realm of thought and prayer.

My forays into this rarefied space have led me to the conclusion that the air up there is too thin. The brain needs plenty of oxygen to work at its best. The confession that theologians, like all human beings, stand on the ground, at a definable time in history and place in geography, is a central contribution of liberation theologians in our day. It is also what makes liberation theologians so dangerous to the institutions, secular or ecclesiastical, that benefit from the present allotment of power. It is why the insights and methods of liberation theology, which I discuss in the Introduction, are so appropriate for gay men, who are excluded from that allotment of power. An ethereal theology, by refusing to engage the structures of domination, conspires to leave them untouched. This is the price demanded for respectability in the academy. It is a price I am unwilling to pay.

My first confession inevitably requires a second. This book is a contribution to a gay, white, male (GWM, to use the shorthand of personal ads) theology of liberation, nothing more. I cannot claim to speak for lesbians or gay men of color. Much of our experience is shared, still more is familiar, but much remains distinct if not estranged.

All the same, I want to acknowledge the enormous debt I owe to lesbian and other feminist theologians. My understanding of my gay male experience has been significantly altered by listening to women and reading women's reflections on their own experiences. Therefore I hope that what I have written here will have some meaning for my sisters in the journey, even as I confess that my tasks are different.

Third, another coordinate, geographic in the literal sense, should help you plot my location. I am a midwesterner, bred in Iowa and a Michigan resident for the past ten years. I have acquired nearly all my experience of gay male life and organizing away from the metropolitan centers of gay life in the United States: New York, San Francisco, and Los Angeles. The lives of those of us who reside elsewhere, especially those who also live away from the smaller "gay ghettos," diverge in a number of ways from what is usually depicted as gay men's culture. I suspect there are more gay men in my situation than in all three cities named, so I make no apology for writing from the geographic, if not the cultural, center of our country. (That I have no ties to the political center will be perfectly clear.) I mention it chiefly because it may explain some of the omissions readers will surely notice and deplore. Because of my relative access to middle-class, white power, however, what I have to say may contain lessons for nongay readers who are struggling with what it means to be both committed to liberation and entangled in the U.S. empire.

Fourth, a confession of where I stand in relation to the church (in my case, the Roman Catholic Church): I knew myself as a gay man before I knew myself as a Christian. This priority of commitment remains at the heart of my life as a member of the body of Christ. I joined the church not in spite of my gayness but because of it. The church, when it is most fully church, is a community where the word of liberation is spoken and acted out in terms of the wholeness of body and spirit; or, in more traditional theological terms, the church is the continuity of the incarnate Word. Just how seriously I take the "carnality" of incarnation will become plain.

Put another way, being Christian for me is very much like being gay: something not so much decided as discovered, then (and only then) chosen. I resisted, and continue to resist, the discovery that I am Christian more than ever I did the discovery that I am gay. The latter was natural, inevitable, and for the most part, painless. But the churches have generally sided with—indeed, been in the vanguard of—my oppressors. Nevertheless, I was claimed by a presence, a Shekinah, and being Christian was the undeniable result. I must add that the Shekinah is loving, not stern, and she claimed me without calling on me to renounce my gayness in any way.

Fifth, I confess that I have used a more individual, personal voice than is just. It is only honest to acknowledge how much I have relied on personal judgment. Carter Heyward, the lesbian liberation theologian who has been a continuing inspiration to me, has written: "If theology is to be worth its doing, we do it at some risk, both boldly and with a humble awareness that our perceptions and images are limited by the boundaries of our own experiences in the world, which are always, to some extent, parochial, irrational, and infused with a certain dogmatic sense that we are 'onto something' important that seeks expression."[2]

At the same time, this book is no more than any other a purely individual achievement. It is the result of much that has been done, said, and written before. That, after all, is the real meaning of "tradition," which we Catholics claim as a source of theology. Many of the ideas and interpretations I offer came to me from others. All too often I could no longer connect individuals with particular insights. Other ideas came to me as "my own" as the result of reading or hearing or remembering bits and pieces that my mind was finally able to make sense of only much later. Where I could identify a particular contribution, it was usually because I read it in a book that I could go back to; in such cases, I have used direct quotations. My reliance on these will, I hope, be taken as a kind of first fruits offered back to those who have brought me here, including, or perhaps especially, those who are not credited.

This manuscript was complete before I managed to get a copy of the Quebecois theologian Guy Ménard's book on this same subject, *De Sodome à l'Exode: Jalons pour une théologie de la libération gaie* (From Sodom to the exodus: Groundwork for a gay liberation theology). I have not yet been able to assimilate Ménard's work fully, much less incorporate his insights into my own. As far as I could discover, this important theological exploration has not appeared in English.

I cannot close without offering some explicit thanks. The first draft of this book consisted of transcripts of a Lenten series of lectures I gave in 1988 at the University of Missouri Newman Center, as the result of arrangements made by the Columbia Catholic Worker community. Their invitation gave me the opportunity to put my ideas in some logical form, and all of them deserve my most profound thanks. I offer the result in loving memory of Lois Bryant.

Kathryn Stern, a valued and valiant comrade, transcribed the tapes of those lectures, thus sparing me the horror of having to begin to write a book with a blank piece of paper staring back at me. What is more, her comments, ideas, leads, and continued support for the project have kept me from abandoning the effort. The American Friends Service Committee's policy of offering staff a three-month sabbatical after six years of service allowed me to put Kathryn's transcripts to use.

The congregation of the Episcopal Church of the Incarnation, Pittsfield Township, Michigan, of whom Kathryn is one, have continued to nudge me in the direction of finishing. In particular, I thank Penny Ryder, Donna Ainsworth, and the Reverend Joseph Summers for their continued interest in this project.

Robert Ellsberg, editor in chief at Orbis Books, took an interest in the manuscript at a critical stage. His labor in promoting it is deeply appreciated; his praise, even more so. The editorial staff at Westminster John Knox have also been immensely helpful. I am grateful for their delicacy in dealing with my touchy authorial sensibilities. I especially want to note their cooperation in dealing with the logistical problems raised by my having returned to live in Japan around the time they first received the manuscript.

Three libraries deserve thanks for enabling a nonacademic theologian to have access to necessary resources. The library of Eastern Michigan University in Ypsilanti is generous in allowing local residents who are not affiliated with the university full use of its collection. I have spent as many hours there as in my own workroom. Another remarkable collection, the Edmund Szoka Library at Sacred Heart Seminary in Detroit, and its predecessor, the library of St. John's Provincial Seminary in Plymouth, Michigan, must be commended for their dedication to the theological self-education of lay people. Finally, the Labadie Collection at the University of Michigan, an archive of scarce anarchist and other radical materials that is especially rich in the area of sexual freedom, has been an invaluable resource for this, as for all my work.

An afternoon over tea with Arthur Evans, who would repudiate the label of Christian theologian, clarified several theological questions for me. I thank him for taking the time to help, as I do Eileen Hansen for arranging the meeting, along with other kindnesses.

Warren Blumenfeld, writer and activist, deserves and here is offered an apology. His pointed wit (grounded in equally sharp perception), his support and concrete advice for my writer's jitters, and above all, the warmth of his companionship are gifts that I treasure and miss.

Some even older debts: my first steps toward looking at these questions from this angle were taken in 1986, during a summer vacation spent with my sister and brother-in-law, Ann and John Bailey, in Port Townsend, Washington, and adjacent waters. Their hospitality and the space they left me for such antisocial activities as reading and note taking I remember fondly, and I here make public my gratitude to them.

Charles Cleaver's generosity, including the wherewithal for trans-Pacific phone calls in moments of discouragement, laid the material foundation for completing the manuscript. He also gave up his time to share with me the secrets of his limpid English style (he bears no responsibility for my failure to use them properly). His partnership with my late mother, Sara Ellen Dever, in producing and raising me might be said to have laid a prior and more basic material foundation. Certainly, without their loving support and their deep commitment to justice, I might never have grown in the knowledge of my gayness as a political fact, which is the seed of this book.

I dedicate this book to a remarkable, unwavering, and matter-of-fact ally, Michael Sprong, who would not let me dedicate an earlier book to him. This time I give him no choice.

Mike and I shared a bitter winter in the rectory of St. Mary's of Rosemount in Warren County, Iowa. One of our neighbors, Bertha, came by every Saturday afternoon to prepare the sanctuary for mass (and dance a little while doing so). Bertha was a storehouse of practical information about farm life. As I wrote this, I often recalled one thing she taught me. She used to sow lettuce and radish seeds on top of the snow in late February or early March. As the snow melted, the seeds planted themselves in the wet soil. Other folks thought she was crazy, she said; but Bertha and her husband Sylvester were always the first in the parish to have fresh lettuce and radishes in the spring.

These pages are like that first lettuce.

Ypsilanti, Michigan
Feast of Saint Waldef

A Note on Using Scripture

I have a beautiful Japanese bowl. It is mended where it once broke. I once saw some new pieces of the same ware in a shop, and they were not so beautiful. The glaze seemed too shiny. My first reaction was to denounce the debasement of a fine old craft. On consideration, I realized what was different was not how the bowls were made. My bowl has been used, and that has given it the rich glow that the new bowls lacked. Even being broken has not harmed either its beauty or its usefulness. Japanese traditionally have treasured priceless old tea things that have been broken and repaired with gold; the place where they were broken now gleams proudly, and the utensil is even more valuable.

This is the spirit in which Christians should approach scripture. Its beauty and value come from being used, even broken. In the liturgy of the Mass, we balance the breaking of the Word with the breaking of the bread. Unless we live with scripture, even risk breaking it again, as I do with my broken bowl, it will have no meaning for us.

I have chosen to use the New Revised Standard Version (NRSV) for most of my quotations. I chose it because, of the readily available versions, it is the one that has most consciously tried to avoid translating into sexist language. It does contain some exceptions to this that make me uncomfortable, however: for example, traditional phrases such as "the Son of Man" and "the kingdom" and, above all, the convention of rendering the Hebrew name of God as LORD. If I were preaching or reading aloud, I would quietly alter them, as I did when these chapters were lectures; but for copyright reasons, I have retained them in print. In as many places as I could, I tried to find ways to avoid this unpleasant necessity. In one place, clearly noted, I have preferred the rendering of the New American Bible, the translation appointed for use at mass in the Roman Catholic churches of the United States.

Although I generally prefer to quote scripture as it is commonly heard in public worship, at a few points I have returned to the original languages. In the case of Greek originals, I am on firm ground, since my academic training was in classics. In one case, the beginning of Genesis, I have pressed my rudimentary Hebrew into service.

I do not pretend that this catch-as-catch-can procedure meets the needs of serious scholars. One goal of my theological project is to reclaim the interpretation of scripture for those of us who are not professionals. We must take the Word as we hear it read aloud in worship or as we read it with the very basic notes found in Bibles published for mass circulation.

One reason fundamentalism has gained so much ground among North Americans—not, of course, the only reason—is precisely that it seems to allow people who are not members of a scholarly elite to reclaim the Bible as their own. My quarrel with this brand of evangelical Christianity is not that (in theory) it leaves biblical interpretation to the masses. What we imprecisely call "fundamentalism" in the United States is two different things involving different casts of characters. On one hand, fundamentalism is a theological point of view. On the other, it is a social movement. The goals of the latter are not necessarily the same as those of the former. This social movement is fundamentally not about interpreting the Bible but about preserving existing power relations.

Beneath its populist cloak it conceals an authoritarian message. Part of this message is that "militant homosexuals" are out to overthrow our social system. A lazy reading of the Bible is the principal means of sounding the alarm. To reach those for whom "the plain meaning of God's word" is hatred of homosexuality, we must offer not elaborate analyses in form criticism or research on the lexicography of Hebrew, Aramaic, and the Koine (important as those tasks are) but an equally direct reading of "the plain meaning" of the gospel of love. That is what this book is intended to provide.

Announcing the Jubilee

> Even the man who has entered the theological circle
> consciously and openly faces another serious problem.
> Being inside the circle, he must have made an existential
> decision; he must be in the situation of faith. But no one
> can say of himself that he is in the situation of faith. No one
> can call himself a theologian, even if he is called to be a
> teacher of theology. Every theologian is committed *and*
> alienated; he is always in faith *and* in doubt; he is inside *and*
> outside the theological circle.
> —Paul Tillich, *Systematic Theology*

What must I do to be saved? This is the perennial
question of Christian life. The preaching church has answered it in
a rich variety of ways over time, although the twentieth century has
shown a preference, not surprising when technology is lord, for
quick and easy formulas.

In this book I take the question apart so that we can look at the
identities of "I" and the complexity of "saved."

Many Christians reading this, especially but not only straight
ones, may wonder why a whole book is needed to answer this
question where lesbians and gay men are concerned. For these
readers, the answer is simple: stop being gay. (The answer from
non-Christian lesbians and gay men is equally simple: stop being
Christian.) There are actually two versions of this prescription. One
is the literal version: turn your life over to Jesus, and you will no
longer be gay. God will deliver you from this lifestyle. The racket
known as "ex-gay" ministries is built on this foundation.

Liberal Christians have come up with a subtler version, failing to
recognize it as really the same. Indeed, they seem to regard it as a
more compassionate alternative to the fundamentalist program,
which they, too, oppose. You cannot help being gay, liberals point
out, and there is no way you can change it; it is something you must
bear, with the help of the church and the sacraments. Under no
circumstances, however, may you "do" anything about it. This
formula is based on a false dichotomy between being gay and acting

gay; it assumes that "acting gay" is merely a matter of sexual activity in the narrowest genital sense. (These Hellenistic dichotomies between being and acting, knowing and doing, and the like are part of what liberation theologians are working to overcome.) But gayness is as much a matter of culture as a choice of sexual object. I look at this reality and its ramifications in the pages that follow.

First, however, that question: What must I do to be saved? In fact, this way of asking the question, common though it is in sermons and tracts, is found in the Christian scriptures only once, in Acts. The Jesus of the Gospels is not a preacher of salvation but one who (as we see in the next chapter) goes about announcing the jubilee, the year of justice and restoration. So in the Gospels we find a different question: What good deed must I do to have eternal life? Living, not safety, is the prize.

There are two instances in which Jesus is asked this question. Both are worth looking at, since his answers are very different from the kind of individualized formula I have described.

Who Is Good?

The more straightforward of the two situations is this (Matt. 19:16–22): a rich young man came to Jesus and asked him what he had to do to "get the life that lasts forever," to give Matthew its baldest translation. Jesus suggested keeping the commandments. The youth claimed to have kept them all his life. Jesus then instructed him to sell all that he had and give it to the poor and then—notice the sequence—become a disciple. The young man just walked away sadly, "for he had many possessions." Even eternal life is not worth *everything*.

There is another aspect to this story, though. All three tellings (Matthew 19, Mark 10, and Luke 18) contain a saying of Jesus about "goodness." In Matthew, Jesus is responding to a question about "good deeds," whereas in Mark and in Luke, Jesus himself is addressed as "good." In each case, Jesus dismisses the notion of goodness as irrelevant, being an attribute only of God, not of any human being or action.

This is almost a throwaway line, but it directly contradicts the approach taken to the presence of lesbian and gay Christians in the churches today. Whichever version of the rules is prescribed, the implication is that the individual gay man or lesbian must become "good" and only then can be considered Christian. Let it be noted that this is not true of a banker or a soldier. When Jesus is asked, "What must I do?" he dismisses the notion of individual goodness and speaks about social responsibilities.

These are not just the usual social responsibilities, either. In all three versions, the story is followed by a discussion that ends with Jesus praising those who have left their families, homes, and conventional responsibilities to follow him. This is much like the answer he gave the rich young man. If you give away all your goods to the poor, you are hardly in a position to take care of a family— and note that Jesus did not say to make provision for them first. Jesus' approach seems to threaten family values as much as lesbians and gay men are alleged to.

Jesus' plan of salvation, to use the language of tract writers, is even more subversive in the other story associated with this question (Luke 10:25–37). Jesus told this parable in answer to a lawyer who Luke (the only evangelist to use this tale) tells us was moved not by genuine concern but by a desire to trap Jesus and cause a scandal. If this was the lawyer's intention, then Jesus walked deliberately into the trap, because the parable is a scandalous one: the parable of the good Samaritan.

We are so used to this story that we have fallen into the Sunday school habit of thinking of it as the story of the *good* (Samaritan) as opposed to the (good) *Samaritan*. But goodness as such is never talked about in the story. Jesus told it to answer a more concrete question: Who is my neighbor? in other words, Toward whom do I have social responsibilities?

Many illustrations could have been given in reply to this fairly conventional question. Indeed, the scripture expert (the meaning of "lawyer" in this context) may have posed it to locate Jesus among the various schools of Jewish interpretation then in flower. But Jesus answered by turning the whole question upside down. His parable directs our attention not to the man who was robbed, the object of our neighborliness (although that is the use to which the parable is put nowadays: to remind us to be good to the needy). Instead, Jesus points to the identity of the person who saw the man as neighbor.

Therein lies the scandal, which our familiarity with the story has bleached out. The model held up to us for imitation is a Samaritan, that is, a rejecter of religious truth and practice; worse, a willful one. To recover the scandalousness of the parable, we might retell it by replacing the Samaritan with a gay man.

Many readers will immediately object that the two cases are not parallel: being a lesbian or a gay man is not like being a Samaritan; it is a deliberately chosen "lifestyle," not an ethnic identity. We will discover in chapters 1 and 2, however, as we examine the nature of lesbian and gay life and identity today, that this is a distinction without a difference. In the present context, it is more important to understand what a Samaritan was to the Jews of Jesus' time: a heretic. Samaritans were not just people from Samaria; they were adherents of a religious system that was in active and bitter conflict with the Judaism of Jerusalem. Samaritans believed that the Jerusalem system had been tainted by Babylonian and Persian influences. By contrast, they "chose a lifestyle" based on rejection of any scripture beyond the Pentateuch, and they centered their worship not in Jerusalem but on Mount Gerizim.

Lesbians and gay men appear even more similar to Samaritans when we learn that sodomy has traditionally been associated with heresy. The English word "buggery" derives from the name of a sect known as Bulgars; under the alternate name of Albigensians, they were ruthlessly exterminated in a thirteenth-century war that amounted nearly to genocide. The medieval historian Michael Goodich, in discussing this association, notes the legal confusion caused (at least for today's historians) by the imprecision of language in the laws of the period.[1]

Jesus does not dwell on the scandal of the Samaritans' chosen lifestyle, though; far from it. He instructs us to "go and do likewise." Go and behave like a Samaritan? Like a heretic? Like a bugger?

Notice who ignored the injured traveler: a priest and a Levite, two religious professionals we might expect to be scrupulous in observing the commandments that Jesus has just summarized in the great commandment to love one's neighbor. Scrupulous they may have been, but their conventional religious training, their "goodness," if you will, did not give them eyes to see the suffering of the mugging victim or did not move them to come to his assistance. But something impelled the Samaritan to act.

Why a Samaritan, exactly? Just to scandalize a smug lawyer? Perhaps; or perhaps to suggest that social choices, not abstract beliefs, are the nub of Jesus' message.

I would like to offer a different explanation. Could it be that the rejection and contempt a Samaritan would have experienced in the Jewish heartland (between Jerusalem and Jericho) made him more aware of violence? Had he too been set upon and beaten by people who recognized from his style of dress that he was a heretic, as lesbians and gay men often are assaulted today by people who believe that by doing so they are cleaning up society? With these questions in mind, let us look again at the parable.

A traveler was going from Jerusalem to Jericho when some muggers attacked him. They not only took his money, they took his dignity too: they beat him up and stole his clothes, then ran away, leaving him half-dead in the gutter.

Soon a bishop came by. He was on his way home after going to Jerusalem to pick up a car given to him by a Cadillac dealer there, who was one of the biggest financial supporters of the diocese. The car rode beautifully, and the bishop particularly appreciated the cream-colored glove-leather upholstery. A little luxurious, perhaps, but after all (the bishop was thinking as he took the curve just beyond Bethany), good quality wears better than shoddy goods. In the long run, what looks like luxury is prudence.

Just beyond the curve, where the road descends to the Jordan Valley, he noticed something piled beside the road. "Litterbugs" was his first thought, but when he got closer, he could see it was a body. He slowed to see more, wondering if he should stop, and noticed that whoever it was had been beaten and was bleeding. He didn't really want blood all over the interior of his new car, but somehow that seemed like a petty reason not to stop. Then he realized that the person was naked. That settled it; it would never do for a bishop to be seen with a naked person in his car. Think of the scandal! Preserving the good name of the church was more important than any passing act of charity, especially in times when the institution was under attack from wild, semi-educated preachers from the backwoods—and trying to keep the goodwill of the colonial administration, too. Anyway, this was a job for the social service professionals. Their agencies got a lot of funding from the diocese. It wasn't as if the bishop weren't helping, indirectly. He drove on.

Fortunately, this being a main route for travelers, it wasn't more than a quarter hour before another car came along. It was driven by a prominent layman, active in the local church and in an organization devoted to restoring religious values to a community that needed them desperately during a period of moral decay and spiritual uncertainty. Noticing what looked like a body beside the road, he too slowed down to find out more. The body, which was bloody and naked, wasn't moving—for by now the mugged traveler had fainted.

The layman, like the bishop, wondered if he should stop and do something. After all, he was someone concerned about his community, not just a person caught up in his own well-being. This might prove an opening to evangelize this poor soul, who, judging from his naked condition, undoubtedly knew not the Lord. But when the person still didn't move, the layman began to have second thoughts. What if the man was already dead? The police would involve him in all kinds of legal red tape. He didn't have time for that; he had more important work. And what if the man lived but sued the layman afterward, claiming he was liable for something or other that happened on the way to the hospital? You couldn't be too careful. Besides, why wasn't the man wearing anything? Robbers don't steal people's clothes. This guy must have done something to provoke the beating. Probably made some kind of disgusting proposition to the wrong person, a healthy if hotheaded young football player perhaps, who did what any man would do in response to a filthy suggestion. Overreacted, of course, but boys will be boys. This guy must have deserved what he got. A God-fearing layman like himself couldn't be going around with low-life scum; it would drag the reputation of his lay ministry through the mud.

The promoter of religious values drove on, too. This time it was only a few minutes before the next person happened by.

A certain gay man was returning home after having been summoned to his head office in Jerusalem. He had been fired because of a rumor that he was gay. As he drove, he wondered if he should have denied the rumor. No, he decided, it wouldn't have done any good. The truth would have come out anyway, when he went into court to testify against the gay-basher who had beaten his lover to death last month. Unconsciously he rubbed the dent in his own skull left by a similar incident he had suffered three years previously.

Suddenly he noticed what looked like a body beside the road. Stopping the car, he jumped out and rushed to look. A naked man, covered with blood and bruises. They looked a lot like the ones he had seen on Adam's body when he had found him in the alley outside their building. Obviously, this man too had been mugged, and judging from the fact that the muggers took all his clothes, the gay man figured it couldn't have been a simple robbery. He felt for a pulse: the man was still alive. Adam had not been; there had been nothing left to do for him. He was being given a chance to make up now for his helplessness then.

He rushed back to his car, returned with the first-aid kit, and did what was needed to transport the man safely. Then he drove him to the nearest emergency room. Because the man had no clothes and there was no way the admissions clerk could tell whether he had insurance, the gay man wrote a blank check to the hospital and promised to come back the next day to clear up whatever else might need to be taken care of.

Later, the newspapers got hold of the story and came to interview him. The bishop read the story and called a press conference, at which he announced that the diocese was giving its Good Samaritan Award to the man who had helped the mugging victim he himself had driven past.

At the award banquet, held at the episcopal palace, the bishop stood with his arm around the Good Samaritan and gave a little homily about showing mercy to our neighbor in distress. This act, he concluded, showed a true Christian spirit. He turned to the man and shook his hand, adding, "God will bless you abundantly for this."

"Oh, I didn't do it for religious reasons. It just seemed like the human thing to do. I haven't been to church since my priest refused me absolution when I confessed I was in love with the redheaded guy who was captain of the wrestling team." The gay man smiled at the cameras.

The bishop was trying to figure out how to deal with the question he knew was coming next.

Could this parable, far from being a conventional tale about the importance of loving our neighbor, be telling us instead that it is to the oppressed, the heretic, the bugger that we must go for teaching, rather than resting in the conventional pieties dispensed by the usual professionals? Can Jesus be saying that suffering oppression brings understanding that the religiously "good," who are revered in society and thus immune from the reality of hatred and violence, can never share?

Such a suspicion is reinforced by the parable's location in the order of Luke's narrative. It is preceded by a passage where Jesus tells the disciples that the truth is hidden from the (conventionally) wise (Luke 10:23–24). It is followed by one where Jesus not only challenges the categories of ethnicity and religious status, as he just has in receiving the report of the seventy and in the wisdom-of-innocents passage, along with the parable of the Samaritan, but breaks the rules of gender as well (10:38–42). Here, in the story of Martha and Mary, someone who has been considered unfit to receive religious teaching—a woman—is welcomed by Jesus. This complements his lesson that heretics have more to teach us than priests and Levites and experts in the law.

Doing Our Own Work

In my discussion of the good Samaritan, readers will have noticed the influence of the Latin American theologians of liberation. For many of us who are tempted to leave the Roman Catholic Church in despair over our treatment there, the theology of the oppressed in Latin America is a rare sign of hope. It reminds us that Catholicism is a living tradition that we can draw on in our struggle for justice, and it demonstrates the possibility of renewing the church itself. We see this in the ongoing realignment of the Catholic Church's political allegiances in many countries. We see it in the explosion of lay ministries and in their revitalizing effect on liturgy, evangelism, and religious life. We see it in the reclaiming of indigenous cultural expressions of spirituality and in the popular canonizations of new heroes of the faith, such as the martyred archbishop of San Salvador, Oscar Romero.

But Latin American Catholics do not only offer us hope; they also challenge us North American theologians. By "us," I mean you, reading this, as well as me, writing it. Elizabeth McAlister, the radical Catholic activist, has pointed out that ours is such a consumer society that we consume liberation theology as if it were some kind of imported Latin American coffee. The alternative, getting down to work and doing theology ourselves, would mean engaging the suffering that must produce it.[2] It is cheaper to buy it wholesale.

One reason, perhaps, is the reluctance of many North Americans to look closely at the oppression in their midst. It is less draining to confront injustice a tad farther from home. This is a luxury I do not share, living as I do in a society that assumes everyone is heterosexual—or should be. Unfortunately, too many lesbian and gay male Christians seem to accept this "should be." This may be one source of my impatience with how lesbian and gay issues are discussed in the churches. The fact of the debate is good. Its substance is the problem.

First, it has tended to be an apologetic debate. I use the word "apologetic" in both its meanings. In technical, theological language, it means rebutting falsehoods, which is a proper task for theologians. But the debate is also apologetic in the common meaning of the word. By this I mean that we have spent too long arguing, "Well, you know, we're really nice people, and we think you should be nice to us and just pretend we're not here and pretend that our lives are no different from other people's lives, and then everything will be fine." It is important that we understand our experiences better, both those that are different and those we have in common, but it does not follow that everything will automatically be fine. What is worse, such a hat-in-hand approach assumes we have nothing of our own to offer the rest of the church. It ignores the gifts that we can bring to the Holy Banquet, gifts that are the fruit of our difference. It reduces us to beggars at the gate.

Real theology means making sense of our differences in the light of our faith in the risen Christ. What do they mean? What do they not mean? What do they teach us about God in Christ, about humanity, about the rest of creation?

The path of apologetics has led to a dead end. So has the other path we have been following. We may call it the scholastic path. By this I mean pulling a word from scripture here and a phrase from scripture there, then arguing about what the words meant in Greece in the fifth century B.C.E., versus what they meant in Greece in the third century B.C.E., versus what they meant to Jews in the Diaspora in the first century C.E., and so on. This is history; it is not theology.

I do not deny that the scholastic approach has uncovered some useful information. But it puts the emphasis on the past. It has failed to engage what we mean now when we call ourselves "gay." The churches should be grappling with that question, as well as with the nature of the society that produced us, the functions of gender in that society, and the functions of repression and homophobia. While philology may help us to see how others dealt with similar questions in other times and places, it cannot do so until we are a lot clearer about the present.

The daily experiences of lesbians and gay men in their historical and political context have not been allowed to enter the debates in the churches. We have been silenced. One weapon that enforces our theological silence is objectivity. Lesbians and gay men are presumed to be incapable of doing theology "objectively." We are considered tainted witnesses because we have an interest in the outcome. For example, when one Protestant denomination set up a study commission on whether to amend its Social Principles with respect to "homosexuality," there was fierce opposition to having open lesbians and gay men on the commission. It would prejudice the results, opponents claimed. They failed to see, or refused to admit, that they too had an interest in a particular outcome, that is, the status quo ante. Admitting that would have been admitting that they found the present state of injustice tolerable, if not desirable.

Such a supposed scholarly objectivity in theology is one of the reasons that looking at Latin American theologians of liberation is useful for North American lesbian and gay male Christians. Liberation theology has called into question the whole idea of purely objective theology; indeed, it has called into question the idea of theology as the special province of academically trained experts.

Latin American Models

The Brazilian friar Leonardo Boff, in defining theology as "systematic reflection on faith," reminds us that "faith is convinced that nothing happens by chance. After all, nothing escapes the dominion of God."[3] Such reflection is a task that falls on all of us, as part of being Christian, whether or not we have degrees or ordination. It is a dynamic process, one that will always continue, because by its very nature we will never come to a final set of conclusions.

Gustavo Gutiérrez, the best known of the theologians of liberation, says that liberation theology is "a critical reflection on praxis in the light of the word of God."[4] He describes praxis as the Christian's "active presence in history . . . a commitment, an overall attitude, a particular posture toward life."[5]

Neither praxis nor reflection on it is limited to theologians, and most published liberation theology is the product of a community's life, which pastoral workers, drawing on their academic training, have put into systematic form—sometimes, indeed, too systematic, for academic presentation can obscure the message. A writer who has avoided this trap, perhaps because he is first and foremost a poet, is Ernesto Cardenal in *The Gospel in Solentiname*. Solentiname is a community on an island in Lake Nicaragua, where Cardenal took refuge as pastor at a difficult stage in the struggle against Anastasio Somoza Debayle. In several volumes, Cardenal retells the community-building among the people there, centering on their dialogue homilies.

A model of liberation theology used by many theological technicians has been described by a Jesuit from Uruguay, Juan Segundo, as a "hermeneutic circle."[6] This process has four stages; they form a circle because completing the process raises a new set of questions that in turn sends us on a new journey. I summarize this process here, because I have drawn on it in the chapters to come; and my reflections will, I hope, encourage you to embark on new ones of your own. Only in this way can a gay theology of liberation be created in community.

The circle begins from *experience,* or as Segundo says, "questions arising out of the present [that are] rich enough, general enough, and basic enough, to force us to change our customary conceptions of life, death, knowledge, society, politics and the world in general . . . a pervasive suspicion about our ideas and value judgments."[7] This suspicion is a crucial element. Theologian Dorothee Soelle, describes it this way: "Theology originates in pain. . . . Its locus is suffering or the disregard for life we experience all the time."[8]

The God we worship is a God of history, a God of events in time. Events are made by people and experienced by people. We do not worship a God of scholarship or philosophy, who exists as a set of propositions to be accepted or rejected. What sets the circle in motion is a question that arises from our history, from the suffering and pain that make us suspicious of what we have been taught, because what we have been taught has not helped us make sense of our pain.

This *suspicion* is the second stage. The discomfort it creates in us propels us to the third stage: *we search the scriptures* in a new way, our perceptions sharpened by our suspicions. Searching diligently, prayerfully, we find something that we overlooked before. This something has always been there, but because we were too comfortable in our experience of the world, we overlooked it, content with old verities rooted in social circumstances that no longer exist.

Finally, in the fourth stage, we use the message of scripture—not a new message but a message newly heard—to *interpret the reality* that sent us to scripture in the first place. Our new interpretation of experience will, in turn, be challenged by reality as we continue living and working and praying and reflecting on that work: that is to say, our new theology will be challenged by our continuing practice. Our theology will be especially challenged by change, the change we are working for; or perhaps it will be challenged more deeply by the absence of the change we are working for. Either will set the circle going once again. Our suspicion will continue as long as we have not come to equilibrium.

To make this more concrete, look again at my version of the parable of the Samaritan. My experience (the first stage) is that I am not regarded as having a place in the assembly of believers as long as I do not renounce, in some fashion or other, my gayness. But in my own life, my understanding of myself as a gay man came before my conversion to Christ. This is admittedly unusual; but the fact is, I came to terms with my identity as a gay liberationist before I encountered the liberating power of Christian community. So my experience included neither an agonizing conflict between a prior Christian rejection of gayness and a discovery of myself as gay nor the neat deliverance that fundamentalists promise "homosexuals" once they accept Christ. They would probably explain this by saying that I have not really accepted Christ. If one includes the phrase "as my personal savior," they are right, because, as we shall see, I do not believe salvation is "personal" in the sense in which they mean it, that is, "private."

This gap between my personal experience and the teaching of the church on sexuality and, indeed, on salvation gives rise to a suspicion that the traditional view of who is "good" enough to be a member of the body of Christ is wrong. This suspicion, in turn, leads me to look at the question "Who is good?" only to find Jesus stating firmly that no one, not even himself, is good. In place of goodness (an abstract quality) Jesus puts love of neighbor (concrete acts). More than that, he does so by proposing as a model a heretic, a member of a group denounced by the religious leaders of his time, just as lesbians and gay men are denounced today. This outcast is the only one who can act as a neighbor. What is worse, many religious leaders refuse to do so. This is the third step: we have come to a new and richer understanding of the meaning of scripture.

Out of this grows a new understanding of our present condition: it is lesbians and gay men, not the religious experts, who can hear Jesus' teaching and act on it. We are the ones who can and must work out a theology of "homosexuality," not the ones who hold power in the churches. Notice the emphasis this process places on scripture. Liberation theology takes scripture seriously. Its fundamentalist critics deny this because they use scripture in such a different way.

Part of the difference is no doubt that liberation theology has its deepest roots in Catholic theology, rather than in the nineteenth-century Protestant trends such as Adventism and dispensationalism that gave rise to the doctrine of biblical inerrancy, the root of what is usually called fundamentalism. Catholics have historically seen scripture as one of several sources of genuine theology, the others being reason, liturgy (this is more often implicit than explicit, but it is important, as we shall see), and tradition. Tradition is the sum of our collective experience as church, that is to say, the fruit of generations of praxis. Thus the priority of experience is not a departure for those of us whose theology is rooted in Catholic ways of thinking.

When I speak of experience, I do not limit myself to what might be called physical experience. Our inner experience is equally a source of theology, which, in any case, is not a science in the academic sense. The renowned theologian Paul Tillich begins his *Systematic Theology* with a caution (the epigraph to this chapter is the second part of that caution): "The scientific theologian, in spite of his desire to become a theologian, remains a philosopher of religion. Or he becomes really a theologian, an interpreter of his church and its claim to uniqueness and universal validity. Then he enters into the theological circle and should admit that he has done so and stop speaking of himself as a scientific theologian in the ordinary sense of 'scientific.' "[9]

Theology is, in the classic definition, *fides quaerens intellectum;* that is, a movement from direct experience of God (*fides*) to an intellectual grasp of that experience, so that it may be connected to the experience of other believers. This movement means that our interior experience is an element of our practice. Prayer and action are thus linked.

Theologian Harvey Cox illuminates what I have been saying about the importance of experience from a different angle. Since the Jesus we encounter in scripture is not only a teacher, since his message is not just in what he says but in how he lived, we cannot separate the narrative passages in scripture from the ethical ones.[10] We cannot answer ethical questions by looking for rules. We have to look at the life Jesus led—in other words, at Jesus' practice.

The Tasks Ahead

This brief description is adequate only to suggest the tasks of the theological technician. The rest of this book will, I hope, put some flesh on these dry bones. I want to accomplish two things: one for gay men ourselves, one for the churches in general.

First, I want to help gay men—and if anything I have to say is helpful to them, lesbians—develop the tools for doing theology for ourselves and our communities. I include non-Christians in my definition of our communities, not from a missionary motive but from what is sometimes called "reverse mission." This phrase refers to the work that many missioners who have served in Latin

America do after returning home: using their experience abroad to illuminate the faith, or lack of it, among North American Christians who benefit from the exploitation of Latin America's people and resources. I believe that doing theology from this angle will help us make sense of lesbians' and gay men's history.

Put another way, I believe liberation theology can make a contribution to the field of lesbian and gay studies, if—and only if—we do not limit our audience to Christians. Many people in our communities are consciously anti-Christian or, at least, anticlerical because of their awareness of being oppressed by the churches' structures and by the state with the churches' connivance. Reflecting on such people's liberating activity can be a way of clarifying how action for fundamental change, whatever its inspiration, is an expression of what others oppressed by the same forces continue to think of as God's saving action in history.

Those of us who continue to think of ourselves as Christians bring to the struggle a gift of understanding that we may call our "hermeneutic principle." We know that God is the source of history, although we human beings are the agents of history. We know too that the God of history is revealed most clearly in liberating activity. Thus, wherever we see people being liberated from oppression we see, with the eyes of faith, God at work. This interpretation does not depend on whether the subjects of the liberating action conceive of what they are doing as "God's work." It does allow us who see it as that to see our community as whole in ways the community in action often cannot.

My second task in this book is to provide some of the information that has been missing in the debates in the churches: stories about what the lives of gay men are like and about how we reflect on them. Let me illustrate this with a reflection on church history rather than scripture: the life and writing of Bernard of Clairvaux. Bernard lived in community with other men and shared intense, loving relations with them. This experience directly informed the theological work that brought Bernard the title Doctor of the Church.

It is no accident that a major vehicle of Bernard's teaching was a series of sermons on the Song of Songs, the erotic poem that is also sacred scripture. His reading reflects his experience—outer and inner—of emotional attachments to men. We are accustomed to considering his experience as "mystical," a term that in this context might as well be "magical." This is because we have fallen for the Platonic fallacy that flesh and spirit are completely at odds.

Bernard's life gives this notion the lie. Another of his many works, *Life of St. Malachy,* is based on his personal friendship with Archbishop Malachy of Armagh. It contains a description of their second meeting, shortly before Malachy died in Bernard's arms. Bernard's account makes deeply romantic reading for a modern gay man. "*Oscula rui,*" Bernard says of their reunion: "I showered him with kisses." Geoffrey of Auxerre tells us what happened later. Bernard put on the habit taken from Malachy's body as it was being prepared for burial at Clairvaux, and he wore it to celebrate the funeral mass. He chose to sing not a requiem mass but the mass of a confessor bishop: a personal canonization and, incidentally, an example of using liturgy to do theology. Bernard himself was later buried next to Malachy in Malachy's habit.

For Bernard, as for us today, this kind of passionate love for another human being was an indispensable channel for experiencing the God of love. Like the Cistercian commentator on the Song of Songs, we modern gay men know the transcendent meanings of erotic experience and the ways it can teach us. Many gay men have turned from Christianity to other spiritual traditions, especially nature religions, because the richness of Christian experience on just this point has been concealed from us. But like the mystics, we have refused to sever our physical experience, including our erotic experience, from our interior lives. This body wisdom is one of the anchors of our lives, a pearl for which we have paid dearly in persecution. It is one of the gifts we have to offer to the people of God.

By working on these two tasks, I hope to provide a kind of tentative framework for a theology of radical loving, of "liberating love" in theologian George Edwards's phrase,[11] of love-in-action arising from our reflection on our present condition of oppression as gay men live it daily. I do so by reflecting on multiple passages of scripture as I did on the parable of the Samaritan, letting the passages comment on one another through my juxtapositions and setting them in the context of contemporary gay male life. Chapter 1 lays the historical and scriptural groundwork. Building on the twin foundations of lesbian and gay male American history and the story of the exodus, the reflections describe a kind of spiral extending from personal coming out (chapter 2) to social commitment (chapter 3) and class consciousness (chapter 4), and from there to solidarity and its embodiment in the resurrection (chapter 5). I conclude with some challenges and a eucharistic prayer.

Before dancing this figure, though, I want to make a point about using those parts of scripture shared by Christians and Jews. The traditional Christian use of what it is high time we stopped calling the "Old" Testament (implying, as the phrase does, that God no longer has a covenant with the Jewish people) has been to take it as "prefiguring" the "New" Testament. This means that events such as the exodus are taken as "antetypes" of the "real" history of salvation, which is to be found only in the life of Jesus. The Hebrew scriptures are implicitly or explicitly taken as having been superseded by the gospel.

I raise this point here because this tendency has been very strong in recent liberal biblical exegesis by and about lesbians and gay men. The denunciations of homosexual activity found mainly in Leviticus are too often answered by proposing a dangerous opposition between an old law of retribution (even, in extreme cases, a "wrathful God of the Old Testament") and a new law of love. This way of reading the Bible denies the legitimacy of Jewish history and Jewish religious reflection on history. In other words, the history told in the Hebrew scriptures has no basic meaning apart from Christians' use of it. This is anti-Semitism at its most basic. In a century when lesbians, gay men, and Jews all suffered from the destructive power of the German state, it can have no place in lesbian and gay male theologies.

Ecclesiastical powers who oppose our liberation are equally guilty of this. When the Roman Congregation for the Doctrine of the Faith, addressing liberation theology, says that the true liberation is from death and sin, achieved by the resurrection, it is saying (intentionally or not) that the exodus has no salvific meaning of its own. God's liberating acts in history before the birth of Jesus are just foreshadowings of the real thing, a kind of divine literary device. This is also anti-Semitism.

Therefore, as we look at stories from the Hebrew scriptures and reflect on their significance for lesbian and gay male liberation, we must be careful not to take them out of their concrete historical contexts, as if they were merely legends or antetypes. The sounder approach is to regard them as authentic (whether literally factual or not) acts of historical liberation at God's hands. This is consistent with the living practice of the Jewish people, who gather now at the Passover meal to connect the liberation relived and celebrated in the seder to the struggles of the present.

If my choice of readings has a certain stream-of-consciousness flavor, it is no accident. My approach is the opposite of proof-texting. I believe that almost any passage of scripture could be used to show that lesbians and gay men have a vital place in the body of Christ. I believe this because of an article of my faith that I hope I can lead you to share. It is this: if Jesus, in his passion and death, freely chose to become a victim of injustice, his sharing of our oppression entitles those of us who are still victims of injustice to demand that any pronouncement of scripture or ecclesiastical authority be judged by whether it helps or hinders our liberation, our becoming subjects of history, not victims only.

CHAPTER 1

God Makes a New People

"Only connect . . ."
—E. M. Forster, epigraph to *Howards End*

An incomprehensible event lies at the heart of the good news. Jesus, who was dead—unjustly killed by those in power—is now alive. In a manner of speaking, all of Christian life since then has been about making sense of this paradox. We struggle to understand and live the meaning of the resurrection: Jesus is sovereign, death is broken, and love is the key. We call this "gospel," good news, but what do we mean by that? How is it good?

We can start our search for answers by looking for evidence of how this news was first proclaimed. One clue is in the Gospel of Luke, which shows the brokenness of people and the brokenness of communities, the presence of outcasts and of people who need to be healed, not necessarily physically. Luke 4:16–21 tells us that Jesus began his ministry by going into the synagogue in Nazareth. He was handed the scroll for that day's reading, the scroll of Isaiah, opened it, and read, "The Spirit of the Lord is upon me, because he has anointed me to bring good news to the poor. He has sent me to proclaim release to the captives and recovery of sight to the blind, to let the oppressed go free, to proclaim the year of the Lord's favor."

The message the apostles proclaimed must have been much like this basic good news, with one addition: Jesus was dead and now is alive. Jesus is alive not just as a resuscitated dead body that will die again, like Lazarus, but alive in another way that is part and parcel of this message of freedom. This point is often overlooked. Jesus' triumph is bound up with freedom for the oppressed; Jesus tells us so at the very beginning of his work. After reading this passage from Isaiah, he sat—the posture of a teacher in the ancient Mediterranean world—and said, "Today this scripture [release to prisoners, freedom for the oppressed] is fulfilled in your hearing." For saying so, he was driven from Nazareth.

This is not only good news for individuals. "Good news to the poor, release to the captives" is not individual salvation. Jesus is pointing us toward a social resurrection. The experience of the early church, as we see it throughout the Epistles and Acts, shows this. New communities, new ways of organizing our collective life, rise from dead models.

The resurrection has to have a social dimension among us too. We cannot limit ourselves to preaching personal salvation. To make this dimension of the resurrection real in our own lives, we have to put it in terms of our own social situations, in all their pain and in all their richness.

So, how is this good news for me, as part of two communities, in both of which I am a member by personal commitment—the Christian community and the queer community? To answer this question, we have to look at each community. In chapters 4 and 5, I look at the making of the Christian community. First, though, I look at the making of lesbian and gay community or communities.

Offspring of History:
The Invention of Homosexuality

There is a lot of historical debate about how, and when, lesbian and gay communities formed in North America and Europe. We do not have space to consider the debate in depth, but because it has a bearing on the nature of our communities and thus on how we do theology in and about them, I need to describe it briefly.[1]

The debaters fall into two camps, usually labeled as "essentialist" and "social constructionist." To summarize, essentialists believe that the common experience of men loving men and women loving women in all times and in all places is more important than variances between cultures, classes, gender and economic systems, and so on. There is enough common about our experience that we can talk about "gay" people in every time and place. Social constructionists, by contrast, say that the societies we live in construct the meanings given to men loving men and women loving women. Because societies are different and have different expectations about human relations, the meanings they construct will be different too. Therefore, to call a man who loved another man in classical Greece a "gay" man is an anachronism. We should use the word "gay" only when discussing the society that gave rise to the concept of human nature and human relations that the word expresses. (It follows that the word "homosexual," the history of which we will examine presently, is a mistaken translation for any word in the original languages of scripture.)

I am not certain that these positions are as distinct as they appear at first glance. To the extent that one must choose, though, I incline to the constructionist view, for two reasons.

First, my own experience teaches me that gayness has different meanings for different classes in the United States. African American gay friends tell me of experiences very different from my own. Living in Japan again after fifteen years' absence, I can see the different meanings Japanese culture puts on intimate relations between men—meanings different enough that it is sometimes difficult for me to know which relations are what we call "gay" in North America. I can also see how the meanings have changed since I last lived here. Nor do we need to look across oceans or years to see how different cultural meanings are given to the same behavior among men and among women. Different places within the United States, and different classes in the same place, read such behavior differently. Lesbian historian Lillian Faderman shows the variety of ways working-class women and middle-class women saw the butch-femme roles lesbians assumed in the 1950s. Gay male historian George Chauncey does the same for what he calls "fairy" and "queer" subcultures in New York at the turn of the century.[2]

Second, for a theologian committed to working from the concrete social circumstances of a given community, the constructionist view seems to promise more. At the very least, it takes seriously the reality of social change and thus the possibility of intentional social change, which lies at the heart of liberation theology. It also helps shift our attention from proof-texting about the past, by either side, to the living experience of lesbians and gay men in this society right now.

In any case, both camps agree that we can trace a continous history of communities of lovers of their own sex leading from at least as far back as the middle of the nineteenth century up through present-day movements in Europe and North America. This history begins with the gradual emergence of an identity eventually named "gay." It will help us to understand this if we look at the history of the concept "homosexual."

The word "homosexuality" seems originally to have been coined by a Hungarian writer, K. M. Kertbeny (originally Benkert), in a pair of pamphlets he wrote in 1869.[3] These were his contribution to a debate over whether to extend the repressive Prussian law against male homosexual activity to those parts of the new North German Confederation with more permissive legal systems derived from French revolutionary law reforms.

This debate was initiated by a lawyer-turned-journalist named Karl Heinrich Ulrichs, from the relatively liberal kingdom of Hanover, which had a less punitive code than that of Prussia. Himself attracted to young men, especially soldiers, he wrote a series of pamphlets in which he tried to figure out why. He came up with a theory that some people by nature were something between a man and a woman: outwardly men but with women's souls. Eventually he decided that some people who were outwardly women had men's souls as well. These people he called *Urnings,* often rendered in English as Uranians; "regular" men and women he called *Dionings.* Much of what he proposed seems bizarre today, but his ideas can't be dismissed outright, for two reasons. First, they called into question, as some of us still do in other ways, the rigidity of the two-pole male/female gender system. Second, they were to underlie the work of Magnus Hirschfeld, of whom I will say more in a moment.

Despite Ulrichs and his allies, however, the Prussians won. Opposition to the harsh law became the core of a sexual emancipation movement at the turn of the century that underlies much lesbian and gay male organizing today.

While Kertbeny's anonymous pamphlets were arguments for freedom of love, his coinage was soon adopted in not a political sense but a medical one and became the name of a disease rather than a liberating concept. The word did not appear at all in English until the 1890s, and it remained unfamiliar in this country even as late as 1920, as we learn from the records of the U.S. Navy's first campaign to eradicate "perverts."[3]

This new concept of homosexuality was adopted as a method of social control by those whose business it was to shape the new social and cultural relations of modern industrial capitalism. In general, their aim was to build a docile class society where individuals could be depended on to carry out their duties to produce commodities for commerce. In particular, the idea of "homosexuality" was useful for promoting the idea that same-sex relations are sick, in connection with two social changes then underway. One of these was the use of medicine to further the idea that people have certain inborn natures. This went much wider than sexuality; it extended to cataloguing different "races," various "criminal" types with distinct racist and class overtones, and immutable "manly" and "womanly" natures, all in the service of capitalist relations.

The other change was an attempt, largely but not totally successful, to create a monopoly of the healing arts by defining medicine as a "scientific" specialty that was the province of men (whose "nature" was more suited to science than women's). Simultaneously, practices such as midwifery in which women predominated were downgraded. This, in turn, was part of a general trend of scientists taking over from religious leaders the role of social standard setters.

The new "scientific" language of homosexuality—which of course, just codified the prejudices of a certain portion of North Atlantic maledom—increased the stigma against intimacy between members of the same sex, an intimacy that (usually stripped of explicitly sexual references) had been commonplace, even idealized, earlier. The result was a new description of men who loved men and women who loved women: sick. I discuss later our eventual refusal of the label "homosexual." For the moment, it is sufficient to note that its widespread use helped direct a shift in the understanding of sexually intimate relations between men and between women from one that concentrated on discrete and forbidden acts to one that described a quality of individuals.

Makers of History:
Organizing and Change

The movement in Germany to repeal the law against male homosexual activity revived in the 1890s. Led by Magnus Hirschfeld, it centered on a petition to Parliament that eventually was signed by some 5,000 people.[4] Because Hirschfeld counted on sympathetic members of Parliament, mainly socialists, to repeal the law, one cannot claim that he built a movement of those he called the "intermediate sex." His greatest contribution was the Institute for Sexual Science. To support his petition drive, he began collecting and publishing material on sexuality from all over the world. The

Institute for Sexual Science fell victim to the first official, public Nazi looting and book burning on May 6, 1933.[5]

In the United States, although there was an attempt in the 1920s to found a Chicago branch of Hirschfeld's organization (the Society for Human Rights), the direct ancestors of today's lesbian and gay movements arose in the late 1940s, most vitally in southern California. Significantly, the first two California groups were made up of people who connected the condition of lesbians and gay men with other forms of injustice, economic and racial. The Knights of the Clock did not survive long, and little has been written about it. It was formed in 1950 as not simply an organization of gay men but an organization of gay men against racism. A former member later reported that its aims were "to promote fellowship and understanding between homosexuals themselves, specifically between other races and the Negro, as well as to offer its members aid in securing employment and suitable housing. Special attention was given to the housing problems of interracial couples of which there were several in the group."[6]

The more durable and thus better known of the two early California groups was the Mattachine Foundation. It was begun by several former Communists and what were then called "fellow travelers" who became acquainted in a music history class taught by Harry Hay at the People's Education Center, a leftist school in Los Angeles. Some believed that any gathering of homosexuals might be illegal, so Mattachine started out as a clandestine organization similar to that of the Communist party.

As the foundation grew and its membership became more diverse, the taint of communism was felt to be dangerous, and the founders were purged. The successor group, the Mattachine Society, had a more conventional structure and took a less radical line. This marks the point where the movement's goals were limited to what would fit inside respectable middle-class society—the very society that defined its respectability by inventing and then stigmatizing "homosexuals."

A lesbian group, the Daughters of Bilitis, was formed a few years later in San Francisco independently of Mattachine. Efforts were being made in New York as well. The movement spread around the country throughout the 1950s.

Although some already took the stance that would eventually be called "gay pride," most notably in the pages of *ONE Magazine,* respectability remained the keynote of this "homophile" movement, to use a favored term of the period. For example, announcements for one Daughters of Bilitis demonstration in the 1960s instructed women to wear stockings and high heels and skirts, lest anyone think they looked too much like the stereotypical lesbian. Despite what gay liberationsists would soon denounce as its conservative tone, however, the movement continued to percolate through society.

It reached me as I was becoming aware of myself as a gay man in the mid-1960s. I found these groups mentioned in the books I read secretly at the local college library, and occasionally the mass media took notice of their existence. Isolated as I was in a small town in Iowa, the knowledge that there were homosexual counterparts to the National Association for the Advancement of Colored People (NAACP) or the Southern Christian Leadership Conference (SCLC) or the Student Nonviolent Coordinating Committee (SNCC) helped me come to terms with my gayness with a minimum of distress.

The increasing militance of these African American organizations, cross-fertilizing with women's liberation and antiwar movements, created historical conditions where lesbians and gay men could envision and then build a movement that relied not on validation by medical and legal experts, as the homophile groups had, but on claiming power over our own lives. The catalyst was the Stonewall Rebellion of June 28 through July 1, 1969, in Greenwich Village, New York.

It began outside a bar called the Stonewall Inn, on Christopher Street opposite Sheridan Square. The Stonewall was not much frequented by the respectable, middle-class gay men of the day. Most of its customers were Latino or African American, most of them were street people, most of them were young, many of them were transvestites. It was the kind of place that was always being raided by the police; in fact, it was the kind of place a lot of respectable homophiles thought deserved to be raided.

On June 28, around midnight, the police raided it again. At first, apparently, folks left as usual, some of them under arrest. Then, for some reason, instead of passively going through the ritual, the customers turned and barricaded the police inside the place and would not let them out. They threw rocks and bottles, forcing the police to call in reinforcements. This led to several nights of skirmishes against police throughout the Village.

Stonewall was a turning point in the history of lesbians and gay men, not only in North America but in Europe. It turned a movement for acceptance and assimilation into a militant movement for "gay liberation." The phrase itself showed the difference: it rejected the medical term *homosexual* in favor of a word we had been using among ourselves to describe ourselves. "Liberation" emphasized not only a different goal but our connection with other movements active at the same time. Stonewall's significance has been so immense as to overshadow the two decades of organizing that made it possible. The significance comes from the fact that it enabled us to begin thinking about ourselves as subjects of history.

Even those of us who lived in places like Iowa were transformed. We began creating new forms of organization to proclaim a new message: we are the ones who will decide what our experience means. We will not wait for doctors and lawyers to tell us. Furthermore, because many of us involved in this new movement had worked on other issues, we had the organizational skills and contacts to take the movement both to the streets and to our wider networks. We could start building a mass movement, reaching beyond respectable, middle-class, white folk, that embodied a sharper understanding of ourselves not just as misunderstood but as oppressed.

In time, this new social reality forced a debate in the churches. Some individual clergy had already begun to call for a different approach to the question of sexuality. In Britain, the Society of Friends had published *Towards a Quaker View of Sex* in 1963, partly because Parliament was considering changes in the laws against homosexual activity. The Quaker pamphlet took what remains a rather radical position for church folk: relationships between men and women, women and women, and men and men should all be treated on a par. In the United States, a few organizations such as the Council on Religion and the Homosexual (formed in San Francisco in 1964) had begun to raise questions in the churches as well. Similar activity was taking place in the United Church of Canada. But it was not until the churches were faced with a new militance after Stonewall that they had to respond.

The Effect on the Churches:
The Terms of Debate

The debate has continued ever since. Though it was necessary, I have not found it very fruitful. In fact, it has become remarkably sterile. I suspect this can be attributed to the fact that the churches are dealing with a new social reality while using an obsolete model.

Their frame of reference is not even "lesbians and gay men," let alone "oppression of lesbians and gay men." Some updating of language notwithstanding, the underlying concept is still "sodomites," individuals unrelated to any other people, and the discrete sexual acts such individuals engage in. The issue of persons with a gay or lesbian identity (parallel to a Samaritan identity), created by the historical process I just sketched, is scarcely to be found in the debate. The closest we have come is a few church statements declaring that a person's identity, if unchangeable, should not be condemned as long as she or he does not "practice" homosexuality. I described this in the Introduction as the liberal version of "stop being gay, and we'll let you join us."

This leaves us two choices. One is to accept the old model and argue about it. By and large, this is what lesbians and gay men have done. They assume those with authority in the churches have been asking the right questions (and you will have guessed by now that I don't believe they have been). We have been content to haggle over the meaning of this or that Hebrew or Greek word in scripture without tackling the larger question of how we read scripture in the first place, much less the even larger question of who the "we" doing the reading may be.

The current path will always lead us to a dead end because, like the homophile movement in the 1950s and 1960s, it relies on experts to define who we are and where we stand in relation to scripture. Even if we get enough experts on our side, which is no longer hard, the church can and does fall back on its authority and say, "This is what we've always taught, take it or leave it."[7] We now even have the edifying spectacle of Catholic experts being disciplined and silenced if their scholarship leads them beyond such obsolete formulas.

The reason the churches have chosen this ground is not hard to figure out. We still believe that sin and salvation are primarily individual matters, unconnected with the state of the world. This is to be expected in a society that values rugged individualism over social responsibility and, indeed, has regressed since the late 1970s from believing that society owes its weakest and poorest members some basic degree of dignity to believing that people are weak and poor through their own fault or through personal choice. The churches have not gone this far, to be sure; but the revival of theologies of private sin and salvation has its roots in this social climate. The churches' retreat into spiritualism may be predictable, but it is not biblical. In fact, the story of Sodom, used so often and so wrongly against gay men and lesbians, stands against any such retreat. Look at how the prophet Ezekiel summarizes the story.

Ezekiel, the prophet of exile, describes the destruction of Jerusalem, past and future (since history is always the present for prophets). In Ezekiel 16, after spending more than forty verses painting the classic prophetic picture of Jerusalem as a wife turned harlot, the prophet says, "As I live, says the Lord GOD, your sister Sodom and her daughters have not done as you and your daughters have done. This was the guilt of your sister Sodom: she and her daughters had pride, excess of food, and prosperous ease, but did not aid the poor and needy" (Ezek. 16:48–49). (Sound like the United States recently?)

Even in a context heavy with sexual imagery, Ezekiel does not describe the sin of Sodom as anything but that classic theme of the prophets: the oppression of the poor.

There are, however, more fruitful and more respectful ways to search the scriptures than picking verses here and there about Sodom. I do not believe that looking for what appear to us to be "gay" or "lesbian" relationships in the scriptures is helpful. Such proof-texting is ahistorical. It fails to recognize that all relationships have different meanings in different cultures; and poor history is bound to be poor theology. It is useless to speculate about whether David and Jonathan or Ruth and Naomi or Jesus and John were lovers. *All* biblical heroes are lovers.

Instead, we must look for stories of people breaking out of the slavery of social and personal relations patterned by gender or class or race or any other category that divides people and allows one group to keep another from full self-determination, from full participation as subjects in history, from full liberation. In the particular case of lesbians and gay men, it is appropriate to look at gender, for we are oppressed because of the threat we pose to the gender system.

Gender Treason

I use the term *gender* to mean the system of social meanings that our society attaches to the biological categories of male and female—categories that Paul tells us in Gal. 3:28 have no more meaning "in Christ Jesus." This set of expectations is woven into a structure of oppression we call "patriarchy." One of the most powerful tools patriarchy uses to maintain itself is the system of homophobia and heterosexism. (By "homophobia" I mean the personal fear and loathing of everything associated with queerness. By "heterosexism" I mean the legal, social, and economic system that codifies homophobia. The distinction between the two is analogous to that between racial prejudice and racism or between misogyny and sexism.) This system keeps patriarchy intact by creating a penalty—the accusation of being lesbian or gay, which carries both a social and a personal price in our society, irrespective of its accuracy—for all who do not conform to the expectations of gender. Men who refuse to kill—conscientious objectors, for instance—are called "faggots." Women who take up "unfeminine" occupations—construction work, for instance—and especially women who do not make themselves sexually available to men are often called "dykes."

We may well ask, Why this particular penalty? One reason is that lesbians and gay men model alternative ways of relating to the nuclear family, on which modern capitalism depends so heavily. I look more closely at that issue later; it is enough for now to point out that some research suggests that gay men who are described as "masculine" are more, not less, disliked by nongays than those who are described as "effeminate." This rather unexpected result suggests that gay men who conform to the stereotype promoted by patriarchy are less threatening than those who do not.

My own history supports this suggestion. It happens that growing up I felt no particular sense of shame or disgust at my affection for and, eventually, sexual interest in men. I recognized that in this part of my life, as in my attitudes toward race and toward war, I was different from the majority but not necessarily wrong. I did wonder, however, what this attraction for men meant when it came to defining myself as male or female. Plainly, I was no female: I lacked the anatomical requirements. By contrast, while I possessed the anatomical requirements for maleness, I lacked two other attributes of manhood that seemed equally mandatory. One was attraction to women. The other was a willingness to use violence. In time, I came to regard this as a gift not a problem. As I began to recognize the injustice embodied in patriarchy, I grew proud of my gender treason.

Understanding gay and lesbian liberation as part of the struggle against oppressive systems of gender was central to the new movement we built in the first years after Stonewall. It remains central for lesbians, although, sadly, it has faded from the thinking of too many gay men. This analysis was an important element of what distinguished the new movement from the homophile movements that had gone before. The first organizations after Stonewall saw themselves as part of the larger movement for liberation in which many of the early activists had taken part and tried (with varying degrees of success, not least because of homophobia in other movements) to work closely with them. This understanding of the meaning of Stonewall underlies my theological project as well.

Thus, the obvious place to begin searching the scriptures for the theological meaning of Stonewall is the classic liberation story, the one all theologians of liberation have turned to: the story of the exodus. It is familiar; so familiar, in fact, that one may well ask what new insights can be drawn from it. As it happens, there are several points that resonate especially for lesbians and gay men. Keeping in mind the caution I raised at the end of the Introduction—the importance of not removing biblical stories from their particular historical contexts—let us turn to exodus.

Coming out of Slavery

You remember the situation: Joseph's brothers, the offspring of Jacob, have settled in Egypt because of the famine in Canaan. Exodus begins with the information that a new king with knowledge of history has come to power in Egypt. He analyzes the social situation: "Look, the Israelite people are more numerous and more powerful than we" (Ex. 1:9). That has a familiar ring. We hear it behind the rhetoric about "illegal aliens" every day. We also hear it in the speeches of Senator Jesse Helms and the Reverend Lou Shelton and Lon Mabon and the other "family values" crusaders of today, with regard to the dangerous power of "militant homosexuals."

"Come, let us deal shrewdly with them," pharaoh goes on, "or they will increase and, in the event of war, join our enemies and fight against us and escape from the land" (Ex. 1:10). Just such a fear is expressed in our society about lesbians and gay men. It was common during the McCarthy period, when the removal of "sex perverts" went hand in hand with the rooting out of Communists. It has been revived in the debate over the open presence of lesbians and gay men in the armed forces.

In Egypt, the result of this fear was first the enslavement of the children of Israel and then attempted genocide. Pharaoh ordered the midwives to kill all the male children. But Shiphrah and Puah, the midwives, obeyed God instead of the king of Egypt:

> So the king of Egypt summoned the midwives and said to them, "Why have you done this, and allowed the boys to live?" The midwives said to Pharaoh, "Because the Hebrew women are not like the Eyptian women; for they are vigorous and give birth before the midwife comes to them." [What a marvelous explanation! One that at the same time excuses and empowers.] So God dealt well with the midwives; and the people multiplied and became very strong. . . . Then Pharaoh commanded all his people, "Every boy that is born to the Hebrews you shall throw into the Nile, but you shall let every girl live." (Ex. 1:18–22)

This expresses clearly the patriarchal worldview: men are the bearers of the bloodline and ethnic identity, while women become part of their husbands' group. If all the husbands are Egyptian, the Jewish people cease to exist. After the exodus, Jewish identity would be redefined, passing down through the mothers, a first step in the destruction of patriarchy.

Next comes the familiar story of the baby Moses, who was floated down the river in a basket and found in the bulrushes by pharaoh's daughter, who raised him as an Egyptian. His mother was made his wet nurse. I feel sure she told him his true identity, but he continued to pass as an Egyptian, living in comfort and wealth at court. He had power; he was, after all, pharaoh's foster grandson.

The time came, however, when he saw an overseer beating a Hebrew slave, "one of his kinsfolk." Then "he looked this way and that, and seeing no one he killed the Egyptian and hid him in the sand" (Ex. 2:11–12). Note Moses' furtiveness. Pharaoh's grandchild likely could have killed with impunity, but Moses was moved by his kinship with the Hebrew; if that kinship were to be discovered, what disaster might follow? Passing means fear of unknown but all-too-imaginable consequences. It means always being vigilant against giving the least clue. How many of our closeted brothers and sisters with access to power have refused to use it for our liberation, have even used it for our oppression, for fear that, by helping, they may be found out!

Moses was found out. The next day, he came upon two Hebrews fighting. "Why do you strike your fellow Hebrew?" he demanded. In this situation, this safe space where there were only Hebrews, Moses let down his guard just a fraction. Solidarity is cheap when it is safe. Moses was told so in no uncertain terms: One of the Hebrews retorted, "Who made you a ruler and judge over us? Do you mean to kill me as you killed the Egyptian?" (Ex. 2:13–14). The sense of a closed group is reinforced by the words: none of us in this conversation is "the Egyptian."

"Then Moses was afraid and thought, 'Surely the thing is known' " (v. 14). So he fled—ran away and tried to hide. In fact, he ran quite a long way, all the way to Midian, where he continued to pass as an Egyptian (old habits die hard), married a local woman, and hoped the whole business would stay hidden. He chose individual safety; perhaps he hoped to find an answer to the problem of being a closeted Hebrew alone, in the desert, lying even to those who had taken him in; or perhaps he hoped to escape it.

Years passed. The king, Moses' foster grandfather died.

> The Israelites groaned under their slavery, and cried out. Out of the slavery their cry for help rose up to God. God heard their groaning, and God remembered [the] covenant with Abraham, Isaac, and Jacob. God looked upon the Israelites, and God took notice of them. (Ex. 2:23–25)

Meanwhile,

> Moses was keeping the flock of his father-in-law Jethro, the priest of Midian; he led his flock beyond the wilderness, and came to Horeb, the mountain of God. There the angel of the LORD appeared to him in a flame of fire out of a bush; he looked, and the bush was blazing, yet it was not consumed. Then Moses said, "I must turn aside and look at this great sight, and see why the bush is not burned up." When the LORD saw that he had turned aside to see, God called to him out of the bush, "Moses, Moses!" And he said, "Here I am." Then [God] said, "Come no closer! Remove the sandals from your feet, for the place on which you are standing is holy ground." [God] said further, "I am the God of your father [i.e., your real father, not pharaoh's daughter's unnamed husband, not Jethro the Midianite], the God of Abraham, the God of Isaac, and the God of Jacob." And Moses hid his face, for he was afraid to look at God. (Ex. 3:1–6)

This gesture is generally interpreted as expressing a "primitive" fear that looking on the face of God is death. I offer another explanation, relying less on superstition and more on psychology. Could it be that Moses is afraid because he is face to face with one who knows who he really is, who sees through his attempt to pass as an Egyptian? We have already been told that when Moses first met Jethro's daughter, he was identified by the Midianites as an Egyptian. He dressed as an Egyptian. He spoke the language of Egypt. Moses had succeeded in hiding his true identity.

This is the strategy we gay men and lesbians know as "the

closet." It is often urged on us by our pastors as a solution to "our" problem. Confessors tell us we should stay away from others of our kind, who are "occasions of sin." If we seek ordination, we are counseled to hide our sexual orientation, since few denominations ordain open lesbians or gay men. Everybody knows that we serve—in numbers exceeding our presence in the general population—in positions of leadership in the churches, as ordained clergy or as musicians or what have you. Still, the disciplines of most Christian bodies demand that this fact be kept secret. Practically speaking, we prefer hypocrisy.

This is worse than dishonesty. It cuts people off from community: the community from whom they must keep secret the truths of their lives and the community that could hear their truths, learn from them, and support them in their pain. It also prevents us from struggling collectively for liberation, our own or others'. It condemns people to the profound isolation that is still, most of the time, the most typical experience of lesbians and gay men in the United States.

To return to Moses: however well he had succeeded in passing, God saw his heart, saw the deception, saw what Moses was trying to do and trying to avoid doing. God saw Moses for what he was, a Hebrew.

No wonder Moses was terrified. Not only was it frightening to be found out, especially after so many years and across so many miles, but it called into question what Moses had tried to make of himself, the shifts and stratagems he had used to avoid facing who he was. To go from being an Egyptian prince to being a Hebrew slave is, after all, quite a fall both materially and psychologically. It is like the fall of many a young lesbian or gay man who has always been the darling of all—because we try harder—when she or he is finally found out as "a filthy pervert unfit for decent human company." Teen suicide related to anxiety over sexuality is shocking, and our society is in denial over it.

God knows us as we really are. No doubt, that is how Moses knew the voice from the burning bush was really the voice of God. He was found out; now there had to be a reckoning. Moses knew it, and so it proved. "I have observed the misery of my people who are in Egypt," the voice went on; "I have heard their cry on account of their taskmasters. Indeed, I know their sufferings" (3:7). God gave Moses the task of ending that suffering. But—and it is characteristic of divine love to combine duty, compassion, and salvation in a single act—God gave Moses the key to ending his own suffering as well. God offered no private solution to Moses' suffering, no "personal salvation," but instead, a common one.

Moses asked for help, for the power that resides in being able to name something:

> "If I come to the Israelites and say to them, 'The God of your ancestors has sent me to you,' and they ask me, 'What is his name?' what shall I say to them?" God said to Moses, "I AM WHO I AM."

God answered with a verb, then continued:

> "Thus you shall say to the Israelites, 'The LORD, the God of your ancestors, the God of Abraham, the God of Isaac, and the God of Jacob, has sent me to you': This is my name forever, and this my title for all generations." (Ex. 3:13–15)

The God who appeared to Moses in this fire is revealed as a God concerned for suffering and for liberation from suffering: the suffering of the people as a whole and Moses' suffering. God offered Moses a path to his own liberation: action on behalf of his people, as opposed to hiding. Moses was not told to work out his salvation alone in the desert, and he most certainly was not told to wait until he had his act together before trying to help others. He was sent back to a dangerous place where he was a wanted man, to work for the liberation of the whole people of whom he was a member.

This path is not unique to Moses. "This is my name forever, and this is my title for all generations," God tells him and us: my name and my nature are the same throughout history. The act of liberation is not a once-and-for-all event—God bringing the Hebrews out of Egypt and that's it, the end of one kind of God and the start of a new one who is convenient and comfortable, who keeps us prosperous and makes everything go along smoothly. That is not the God of the bush that is never burned out.

Moses went back to Egypt, as we all know. Pharaoh's hardened heart was met by an escalating series of plagues, culminating in the death of the firstborn. God told Moses how the people God would lead into freedom were to be marked out, to preserve them from destruction. Notice that this was the first plague that did not affect everyone in Egypt, Hebrews as well as Egyptians. So far, everyone has suffered. Then as now, the oppressed suffer and are willing to suffer for liberation. We learned this from the African Americans in Montgomery, Alabama, who walked rather than patronize a segregated bus system. We heard it from South Africans who called for maintaining sanctions. We were reminded of it in recent events by

Haitians calling for a genuine embargo to restore their constitutional government. Liberation is serious work. It entails risk.

The Hebrews in Egypt, though, had already lived through one attempt at genocide—the killing of all male newborns by pharaoh. Furthermore, God meant to form a new people out of these slaves, so they had to be kept alive. Moses passed on to them God's instructions:

> "Select lambs for your families, and slaughter the passover lamb. Take a bunch of hyssop, dip it in the blood that is in the basin, and touch the lintel and the two doorposts with the blood in the basin. None of you shall go outside the door of your house until morning. . . . You shall observe this rite as a perpetual ordinance for you and your children. When you come to the land [of promise] . . . you shall keep this observance. And when your children ask you, "What do you mean by this observance?" you shall say, "It is the passover sacrifice to the LORD, for [God] passed over the houses of the Israelites in Egypt." (Ex. 12:21–22, 24–27)

Then came the plague and the weeping, and the Israelites were let go.

They were led by a pillar of cloud by day and a pillar of fire by night, until they arrived at the seashore.

> As Pharaoh drew near, the Israelites looked back, and there were the Egyptians advancing on them. In great fear the Israelites cried out to the LORD. They said to Moses, "Was it because there were no graves in Egypt that you have taken us away to die in the wilderness? What have you done to us, bringing us out of Egypt? Is this not the very thing we told you in Egypt, 'Let us alone and let us serve the Egyptians'?" (Ex. 14:10–12)

Longing for Egypt

It always seems easiest to keep still in the face of oppression. Church people are especially apt to prefer order over struggle. Martin Luther King, Jr., discussed this very issue in his *Letter from a Birmingham Jail*. Responding to some local ministers who deplored the presence in Alabama of "outside agitators" in the shape of Christian ministers, King contrasted the transforming power of the early church, when it was still willing to upset the existing relations of power, with its present role as consoler, giving tacit or even overt approval to an unjust status quo.[8]

If that was true of the churches' attitude toward racial justice in

1963, how much more could it be said today of the churches' attitude toward freedom for lesbians and gay men? At best, the response of the institutional church is another study commission; at worst, it is a cynical use of its historical complicity in our persecution to justify continuation of our oppression.

And we gay men and lesbians within the churches, how often have we chosen not to rock the boat, contenting ourselves with that study commission simply because it was not more persecution? How often have we been willing to go along with exempting the churches from gay rights ordinances? How often have we depended on those in power to define our relation to the gospel—preferring the known sufferings of life in Egypt to the dangerous task of building our own future?

God knew the people coming out of Egypt. Scripture tells us that they were led not by the shortcut, along the coast road, but by a route that took forty years. We prefer shortcuts. One shortcut is to say, "We're just like you. We'll get doctors and lawyers to tell you so." Then we prove it by reducing our movement for liberation to a system of commercial products and institutions—bars, publications, gyms, fashions, cruises. This, in turn, means we become accomplices in an economic system that causes untold suffering for others. Not surprisingly, these others fail to see us as comrades in the struggle for justice. We have created a new Egypt, where we can feel as if our liberation has already been won. Such outcomes are inevitable once gayness and lesbianism are conceived of as lifestyles rather than as membership in an oppressed class.

We have tried to buy ourselves out of bondage, a common enough temptation, a bribe capitalism offers to a chosen few members of the groups it oppresses. An analogy, admittedly inexact, could be made to the way class has been neutralized as a revolutionary force in the United States. By increasing the standard of living for the working class without changing workers' relation to capital, the militant unions of the 1930s were, by the 1950s, brought to accept a situation where prosperity for the exploiters has continued to seem necessary for the workers' survival. At the same time, enough space for social mobility has been opened, largely through access to higher education and professional status, to make credible the myth of a classless society.

Just so, white gay men—for lesbians and gay men of color, like women and people of color generally, have less access to this option—have been coopted into believing that they are free if they can afford to live a certain lifestyle. This requires money, which requires steady and lucrative employment, usually as a professional, which imposes self-censorship and atomization on those who choose this strategy. If you can buy yourself out of bondage, you can also be sold back into it when your buying power drops—so you had better live "discreetly."

As a result, class, gender, and race divide lesbians and gay men. This means we can be played off one another and at the same time be kept from forming common cause with other oppressed groups. They, in turn, are kept from forming common cause with us by the stereotype that all gay men are white, rich, and dedicated to our own material comfort. This stereotype was used explicitly in the 1992 political campaigns in Oregon and Colorado to block our civil rights. The propaganda for these campaigns asked people to believe that civil rights for lesbians and gay men are "special rights" for people who already have more than average folks do.

Another example of the long-term problems a strategy based on financial success creates is conflict over housing costs as gay men move into poor neighborhoods (often the only ones we can afford, since banks still routinely regard us as credit risks). We renovate old houses and make neighborhoods fashionable again. This drives up housing costs and drives out the poor who have been living there. Those being driven out, not surprisingly, turn against us, not against lenders or the real estate industry. Thus are the oppressed pitted against one another.

It is easy to feel that gay neighborhoods in the few large cities where they exist are liberated zones where we are free to live without the persecutions we left behind. I'd love to live in the Castro or West Hollywood myself someday. But in fact, they are more like the Egyptian bondage for which the Hebrews pined. The suffering we know has at least the virtue of providing a sense of security. At the same time, we should recall the original ghettos of the Middle Ages. They nurtured a rich and vibrant Jewish culture, but that is not why Jews lived there. They were forbidden to live anywhere else. The ghettos had gates that were locked at night. Then, when a pogrom was in order, Jews could be located right away and slaughtered. The fact that gangs of gay-bashers now know where to find us and travel considerable distances to do so (as trial documents show) demonstrates the shortcomings of looking for safety in Egypt.

Exodus tells a different story: "Moses said to the people, 'Do not be afraid, stand firm, and see the deliverance that the LORD will accomplish for you today' " (14:13). We all know what happened next. The sea was parted, the fugitive slaves passed through on dry ground, the waters flowed back and drowned the armies of Egypt.

> Then the prophet Miriam, Aaron's sister, took a tambourine in her hand; and all the women went out after her with tambourines and with dancing. And Miriam sang to them: "Sing to the LORD, [who] has triumphed gloriously; horse and rider [God] has thrown into the sea." (Ex. 15:20–21)

This, I have been told, is the oldest passage in scripture. If so, it is appropriate that it should be the first utterance of those who before were voiceless. Those who sing it are those who have succeeded, against heavy odds, in preserving themselves in the face of powers that deny their collective identity. Just so, gay men and lesbians have been considered by society and church to be individual sinners, not members of a gathered people. Only now have we begun to sing the song of our peoplehood.

Our song of triumph has not yet been heard by the churches we dwell in. There, we are still "nonpersons" (as Gustavo Gutiérrez describes the poor in Latin America). We must become a people before we can become subjects of our own history, just as the fugitive slaves did in the midst of the exodus.

The Lessons of the Desert

The formation of the Israelites into a people took place in four stages: first, the Passover, marking off people as different; second, the miraculous passage through the Red Sea; third, the covenant on Sinai, when the people marked off at Passover responded to having come safely through the waters of freedom by agreeing with one another that they would be one people and by agreeing with God that they would be a people for God (the covenant is the choosing of peoplehood over individual salvation, over atomization); fourth, forty years in the desert.

All four stages were necessary to form these "nonpersons" into a people. It took forty years of working to do it. The miracle at the Red Sea was not sufficient; it was merely the turning point, the catalyst, the Stonewall Rebellion that made people realize that they had a shared history, so that they could move together toward their own empowerment. That began with their commitment to one another at Sinai.

Forty years were needed so the people could forget the patterns of thinking that kept them enslaved. We have seen this already: "What have you done to us, bringing us out of Egypt?" It wasn't so bad there, at least we had food, at least we had a roof over our heads. Sure, we had to work hard, but at least we knew that the master was going to take care of us, that we would have a meal at the end of the day. Here we are in the middle of the desert, we do not have any water, we don't have any food. Who will take care of us?

We have to learn to take care of ourselves.

We also have to give up worshiping idols. That takes even longer. When Joshua led the people in renewing their covenant at Shechem (Josh. 24:1–15), he said, All right. Take your pick. You can go back to worshiping the gods of Egypt. You'll have to go back to Egypt to worship them, though, and I'm not going to lead you there: "As for me and my household, we will serve the LORD." Nor is that the last choice. The choices just keep coming— especially the choice of whether to identify with the oppressed, of whom you are only one part.

This process has never been finished for the people called Israel. It is only beginning for lesbians and gay men. In both cases, though, it begins with a setting apart, either by blood on a doorpost or, in our case, by medical and legal experts declaring, "These people are this kind, those people are that kind. These are the good ones, those are the bad ones." You have to be one or the other. Choose.

Maybe you do not choose. Maybe, as I am sure Joshua believed, you are chosen. The matter of choice is fiercely disputed when we are promoting our several concepts of gayness and lesbianism, but the distinction between choosing our sexuality and being chosen by it is less clear in real life than in philosophy. It is also less important to how we do theology than we think. We may, after all, choose to become Samaritans. Is that a right choice or a wrong one?

Anyway, this concept of sexual identity as an either-or matter is new, as I have described—far too new for any of the scripture writers to have encountered it, much less taught about it. We need to spend more time thinking about where we got it. We should examine the proposition advanced by Claude Summers in a review of Louis Crompton's *Byron and Greek Love:* "The pervasive homophobia of the late eighteenth and early nineteenth century might . . . itself have helped develop a homosexual identity. However abusive and brutal, the ubiquity of denunciations of sodomites during the period might actually have helped create the feeling of solidarity with others of a like nature that Crompton cites as a constituent element of Byron's homosexual identity."[9] Such a line of development would plainly increase the analogy with the formation of Israel.

However it came about, there is now a division between gay and straight, as there is in Exodus between those passed over by the angel and those whose firstborn died. Those of us on the gay side have a shared history, as those passed over do—one that even includes plagues and attempts to eradicate us. Like Jews (and Communists and Gypsies and so many others), "homosexuals" were marked for destruction by Adolf Hitler in order to cleanse the "Aryan blood" of Germany of all factors in the gene pool that caused degeneracy.

We are still wandering in the desert, trying to figure out what it means not to be slaves anymore. The nonpersons have been formed into a people by the pivotal historical event of Stonewall.

But into what people? The fugitive slaves whom Moses led out of Egypt are formed into God's people. They made a covenant together at Sinai, a covenant with God, a covenant that brought an element of security back into their lives, replacing the false security of enslavement. We know, as perhaps they could not yet have known, that their security also depended on keeping their part of the covenant with God. Ezekiel describing Jerusalem as a harlot was describing a Jerusalem already destroyed. A covenant, being a relationship, does not just happen once and for all. The fugitive slaves who formed themselves into one people at Sinai by their covenant made themselves not just former slaves but lovers.

Creating this related, loving, covenanted people is part of the act of liberation. People are not liberated one by one, as the "buy yourself free" model would have it. Salvation is collective. By covenanting, we choose to be part of a gathered people, a people called out of the undifferentiated mass of humanity. The Greek word for a people "called out" is *ekklesia,* "church."

We know this about the church. We affirm it in the way we talk about being members of one body, the body of Christ. This means, if it means anything, that our humanity is found in our relation to other people. It is a pretty concept. But it is not really part of my experience as a gay Christian. I experience my relation with the rest of the people of God not as belonging but as isolation. And isolation is central to how I experience oppression. It is the form of my oppression. Isolation means that I do not know where to look for others who share my oppression. Silence, masquerading as "discretion," means that I cannot look around the assembly at worship and feel others with whom I can connect on the basis of shared history.

Outside the congregation it is easier (this is the very reverse of how things ought to be). Stonewall made this difference for my generation: it broke down our sense of isolation and replaced it with a sense not only of belonging but of common, self-conscious struggle. We became a covenanted people, journeying through a desert together.

So we celebrate it every year, at the end of June, with parades and film festivals, with workshops and worship, for the same reason that Jews celebrate Passover: to renew ourselves as a struggling people who became, in a moment of history, subjects of history—and yet are still becoming.

CHAPTER 2

Naming and Power

His brain was still feeble, but he was obliged to use it, for so much in current speech and ideas needed translation before he could understand it.

—E. M. Forster, *Maurice*

After they had been brought out of slavery in Egypt and wandered forty years in the desert, a group of outcasts had been formed into a people—not just any people but a special people, a people of God, an *ekklesia,* or church. To use the language of Jesus, we would say they had been formed into a community of hearers and doers of the Word, a group of people who had grasped the message of liberation and learned how to use it to transform the world around them.

How can this be? By the nature of oppression, an oppressed people must be suspicious to survive. How can such a people feel secure enough to listen to any messenger, much less begin to transform the message into some kind of liberating action?

If they are to hear, the oppressed must be able to translate the message into terms that make sense in the circumstances of their lives. Such cultural adaptation of the good news is already present in the Christian scriptures. Saul, by becoming Paul, brought the Aramaic preaching of Jesus to Greek-speakers of the eastern Mediterranean. Paul's work launched the process of translating Jesus' message into the Greek philosophical terms that we have inherited, although we no longer live in the society that gave those terms meaning.

The oppressed cannot do this translating unless they are conscious of their own identity. We must name our oppression, analyze it on the basis of our experiences, not just accept the terms provided by the oppressor. In other words, to expect lawyers and doctors—or bishops and synods, for that matter—to validate us, as the homophile movement did, does not work. We waste our time trying to become respectable enough to be accepted by the majority, as assimilationists do today. Our tasks are harder: analysis and strategy, what nowadays is being called "queer theory." The first and central step is the process we call "coming out."

Now that we have remembered the drama of the people of Israel coming out of Egypt, the phrase "coming out" means something new. In the exodus, as in our lives, it means moving out of a situation of bondage—the bonds in our case being secrecy and silence—into freedom. Israel had to come physically out of Egypt in order to worship God and not the idols of Egypt and also had to come out of the way of thinking that makes it possible for slaves to remain slaves: the habits that make idols seem like gods. There was no way to get free in Egypt. Had pharaoh decreed their emancipation, they would have been more likely to continue worshiping idols, not less. Just so, for us, coming out is the key to our freedom.

Before I Knew My Name

The term *coming out* really covers several choices. It can be thought of as a series of expanding events. I become conscious of myself individually, personally, privately as a gay man. This consciousness may not at first have a name. In my case, not only did it not have the name of pride—"gay"—it initially did not have even the medical term *homosexual*. My consciousness of my love for other males preceded any name I had for it.

This may not be surprising for somebody who was living in a small midwestern town in the mid-1960s. Thirty years later, though, twenty-five years after Stonewall, it has become a commonplace to say that "the love that dare not speak its name" is now "the love that will not shut up." One might well think that contemporary young people have all the information they need to come out painlessly—too much information, many claim.

In fact, young people's lives and testimony reveal that things have changed very little; hence the results of a 1989 study commissioned by the U.S. Department of Health and Human Services, which showed that one-third of youth suicides occur among lesbian, gay, or bisexual young people, and hence, even worse, the successful campaign by right-wing members of Congress, led by

Congressman William Dannemeyer of California, to get Secretary of Health and Human Services Louis Sullivan to suppress that report.[1] This and the controversies in school systems around the country over how to include the stories of lesbians and gay men in curricula demonstrate that powerful forces, often describing themselves as Christian, are determined to make sure that the situation never does change.

Thus, for many people, there is no coming out at all. This raises the question of whether such people can be said to be "gay" or "lesbian." Take the example of men arrested in restrooms for anonymous homosexual acts. There are, of course, open gay men who engage in anonymous sex for a variety of reasons, including the simplest of all: they like it. Commonly, however, the victims of this kind of police entrapment (as it usually is) are married men who desire sex with other men but do not in any other way identify themselves as homosexual, let alone gay, and who certainly do not take part in any aspect of gay political, social, or cultural life. This demonstrates once again that "gay" is a social construct. It makes scientific debate over whether "homosexuality" is a biological trait or a learned behavior irrelevant. Being gay is a choice on the level that actually matters: whether one represses homosexual desire or constructs an identity around it.

This matter arose in 1993 in an overtly political context. President Bill Clinton's announcement of his intention to rescind the military regulation forbidding lesbians and gay men to wear the uniform led to a furious, if rarely very intelligent, debate that ended up centering on how freely lesbian and gay members of the armed forces would be allowed to make their sexual identities known. President Clinton framed the debate as one between "behavior" and "status." Much of the subsequent argument was about whether it is possible to separate the two. Those who argued that it is not fell on both extremes of the debate. Conservatives such as Senator Strom Thurmond, whose position prevailed in the final "compromise," contended that being gay meant that one absolutely does engage—what's worse, is compulsive about needing to engage—in "sodomy," which is illegal under military law. Some lesbian and gay rights advocates, by contrast, argued that it is unjust to require celibacy from some members of the armed forces and not from others.

One may well ask how "gay" a young marine can be said to be if he is not allowed to call himself gay publicly, is not allowed to go to a gay bar or demonstration, is not allowed to express sexual desire for another man, and is not allowed to read gay literature. If this marine took part at some level in the gay subculture before he joined up, he might well be a gay man who has made a decision to suspend his gayness "for the duration." If, as is more common, he joined at seventeen in hope that the marines would make "a man" of him, then discovered he was sexually aroused by his comrades in arms, how is he to give some kind of meaning to that desire—as he must, if he is to live responsibly—unless he can interact with other men who have already learned to do so? What will "being gay" mean to him except fear and repression? How can any useful fruit be cultivated in such rocky ground? What does it mean to say he has "come out"? What has he come out from? Into what? Gayness, in this context, is drained of all social and political content (exactly what supporters of the policy want to happen) and is reduced to a private—indeed, secret—individual consciousness.

This individual consciousness is sometimes a person's only coming out. Once having achieved it, one can repress it, accept it but keep it secret, or join others who have had the same experience. A typical story goes something like this: "Well, I knew that I was different somehow, but I didn't know anybody else felt the way I did. And then I heard about a bar over in the next city, where a lot of people like that go. So I went."

Finding Our Own

Our first experience of being in the midst of others like ourselves is generally even more of a transforming moment than the private recognition and acceptance of our gayness, and it is usually this experience that people call their coming out. Historian George Chauncey reminds us that earlier in our history the phrase "coming out" was restricted to this event. Although we have come to think of it as an abbreviation of "coming out of the closet," Chauncey tells us that it originated without reference to any metaphorical closet, as a parody of the society ritual of the debutante, and meant the occasion when a person was acknowledged by the gay world as a full-fledged member, often marked by a party. My own college friends gave me just such a coming-out party, a bit belatedly, in 1971. Chauncey's discussion of this point emphasizes the social as opposed to the personal (not to say private) character of coming out.[2] Lesbian and gay male literature has always played a vital part in this stage of coming out. This was especially true before Stone-wall.

During the 1950s, the pages of periodicals such as *ONE* or *The Ladder* (published by the Daughters of Bilitis) were full of letters from lesbian and gay male readers who would otherwise have been totally alone. As early as 1870, Karl Heinrich Ulrichs, the German activist mentioned in chapter 1, quoted in his pamphlet *Prometheus* such a letter that he had received: "The poor person who feels this fateful drive within himself, under the ban of world opinion until now, had to consider himself a trespasser of the laws of nature. Under this frightful consciousness all the energy of his soul was crippled. He has you to thank, if now, like awakening from a nightmare, he can breathe again. You have given him back his self-respect!"[3]

Without this stage, it is difficult to move from a consciousness of oneself as "different" to a consciousness of oneself as "oppressed." Such movement comes most often in conversation, in sharing experiences and finding common themes. This process is a (usually informal) version of what the women's movement taught us to call "consciousness raising." (Among U.S. gay men, this has not yet become a deliberate process of building class consciousness. I look at that issue in chapters 3 and 4.)

The last coming out—one that many of us never achieve—is bearing public witness to our existence and to our oppression. This may take a number of different forms. Often it happens the first time we march in a gay pride parade. One reason many lesbians and gay men never take this step is that it can mean burning bridges as well as coming out.

Such public coming out does not happen just once. Whether the witness is widely public, such as being on television, or whether it happens at work, which is both public and limited, it has to be repeated, when we move from one workplace or town to another, for example. We may not be free to repeat it for quite some time, if ever. Almost any new situation requires a decision about how safe it is to be open. Each time I make a new acquaintance, the question comes up: How much will I be able to say to this person about some essential piece of my life? It is not an easy decision. Sometimes I get tired of making it; finding it easier to drift, too often I decide not to decide.

Nevertheless, coming out publicly brings a sense of freedom that must be experienced to be believed. Coming out is one of our many seasons of joy. This is why when gay men sit around chatting, the conversation often turns to our coming-out stories. We tell them and listen to them again and again because they tell us who we are.

Sometimes we can see the benefits of coming out more easily in others than in ourselves. It is like marking the growth of children we see only once a year. I recall a friend. I had known him very well for a number of years, and he always knew I was gay. He always seemed a little uncomfortable about it; from time to time, I found myself censoring my behavior to spare his feelings. Nevertheless, he was—and still is—very dear to me, and we continued to visit each other as often as our circumstances allowed. I can remember sometimes wondering what was going on with him: he seemed to me very isolated, no girlfriends but no boyfriends either. Perhaps his genuine sense of himself was as a solitary, a kind of hermit in the city; he is a person of sufficient spiritual depth to make that a reasonable conjecture. Perhaps his relationship with God was so intense that there was no room for anyone else, except on the level of friendship.

He was visiting me one evening on a cross-country trip. As I look back now, I can see that he took some care to steer the conversation in a direction that let him casually drop the fact that he, too, had come to understand himself as a gay man. Suddenly, I saw him in an entirely new light. I had always thought of him as a person of great wholeness, of great spiritual depth, but now it was as if he had blossomed. A budding rose can be very beautiful, but once the rose is finally open it is completely different and even more wonderful. In that moment, I recognized that up to then I had seen only three-quarters of him. Now I saw him in the round.

One may wonder whether it was he who changed or my perception after hearing his news. Probably the answer is some of both. In any case, this experience showed me what coming out can do.

There are a lot of social barriers to coming out—some enforced by the heterosexual community, some by ourselves. The most important is invisibility. Invisibility requires what is sometimes called the "heterosexual assumption." It is remarkable how many people believe they have never met a lesbian or a gay man. They probably have, but they overlooked the person's gayness, brushed it under the rug, whether consciously or not. We are expected to assume that everyone we meet is straight. If the heterosexual assumption proves false, a second form of invisibility kicks in, usually known by the euphemism "discretion." "Let's not raise these unpleasant issues here." (Unpleasant for whom?) "We're not going to pry into their private lives." (I talk about private lives later.)

Another, internally generated enforcer of invisibility is the fear, quite common among lesbians and gay men, of losing the friendship of someone dear to us. Most of us have had this happen once or twice, often enough to plant the possibility ineradicably in our minds; hence the need to decide when and how to come out to other individuals. My rule for myself, in theory anyway—in practice I am far from consistent, of course, and often drift—is to announce myself early in a relationship. This strategy risks having people think I consider being gay the most important fact about myself. This is often what is meant when people accuse us of "flaunting" our gayness. The concept of flaunting, of course, depends on the heterosexual assumption: we do not call wearing a wedding ring "flaunting" heterosexuality. However unsatisfactory it may sometimes be, early disclosure provides an early warning. It lets me gauge right from the outset how much to invest in a relationship, before I get in too deep.

The Costs of Coming Out

Sometimes all this is dismissed as personal indulgence. A phrase some leftists use to describe the situation of lesbians and gay men is "psychological oppression," implying we are dealing with feelings and interpersonal relations, not with structures of oppression. I look more closely at this issue and at how lesbians and gay men are exploited in the narrow sense of the word below. For now, it is enough to point out that there are concrete economic and personal consequences to coming out.

In 1987, for instance, I worked on the civil disobedience at the Supreme Court that capped the October March on Washington for Lesbian and Gay Rights. (The march itself was on Sunday, and the civil disobedience was on Tuesday.) One of my tasks on the morning of the action was to connect people with affinity groups. I had folks tell one another something about themselves so that they would not be arrested with total strangers. One man said, "I guess the thing I most want to share is that when I came down for the weekend, I didn't tell anybody at work why I was coming to Washington. I was so moved by the march that I decided to stay for the civil disobedience. When I called my boss yesterday morning to say I needed two days off, he said, 'I know why you're in Washington. I read the papers, so don't bother to come back.'"

One of the most painful consequences of coming out is having our children taken away. Lesbians suffer most often from this; lesbian mothers can be denied custody of their children if their lesbianism becomes an issue in their divorce. But I have known gay men who were forbidden to see their children. This is how we are treated by a society that denounces us as "antifamily."

The churches are a major obstacle facing gays and lesbians. Many of us abandon our churches, sometimes in great sorrow and anger because they have meant so much to us. Others come to the church for guidance and help. Asking for bread, they get a stone. Many Catholic pastors tell those who turn to them, "It's not so. This is just a phase, don't think about it, don't worry about it, just think about girls (or boys) instead." Another common bit of advice, as I noted before, is "Avoid the occasion of sin. Repress your impulse to love other people. It's an intrinsically disordered impulse;[4] keep it in check. Stay away as much as possible from people you might want to be in love with: avoid the company of other lesbians and gay men." This keeps us isolated and cuts us off from any opportunity to learn from others how to make sense of our lives.

One of the worst prescriptions is marriage. How often and how recently it has been used I cannot say, but anecdotes abound among gay Catholics. I know of one case directly. A friend's mother married a man she did not know was gay. His parish priest had apparently told him to marry her and she would make him straight. Needless to say, the marriage did not last. The suffering for both parties can only be imagined. My friend's mother left the church.

This experience of alienation is encapsulated by the English gay novelist E. M. Forster in the epigraph to this chapter. It reaches from society into the church—which we have been brought up to believe is the body of Christ of which we are all members, which we are taught can restore our sense of wholeness—and presents us with a contradiction.

It is no surprise that whether we leave or stay, we react to the church with suspicion. Something about what the church is teaching, indeed, something about how the church conceives itself, is not right. In the case of the church's relation to gay men and lesbians, we can dissect out two particular explanations for this suspicion.

First, the church has allowed itself to subordinate the commandment of love to the demands of heterosexist culture, defying Paul's injunction "Do not be conformed to this world, but be transformed by the renewing of your minds" (Rom. 12:2). This is partly the result of the general deformity that political theologian J. B. Metz has described as "bourgeois religion" (I look more closely at this term in chapter 4). It is also partly and, perhaps, more directly the result of the churches' long-standing obsession with sexual activity. This well-known obsession leads to a reduction of the lives of lesbians and gay men to the realm of sexual experience. A counter to this reduction is the observation that Antony Grey, a British gay rights activist, made thirty years ago: "To many people, the most shocking thing about homosexuality is that it is about love. (This is the most shocking thing about Christianity too.)"[5]

I deliberately introduced here Paul's warning in Rom. 12:2 against conformity to the spirit of the age, because in the debate over the place of lesbians and gay men in the churches, it is often the text used to excuse the ecclesiastical status quo. The argument goes something like this: "This is just a passing fad, a sign of the degeneracy of the world around us. Allowing lesbians and gay men to participate openly in the life of the church is just conforming to the immorality of the age. We mustn't allow the contemporary fashion of being nice to lesbians and gay men to deform the eternal teaching of the church."

I find this contention that the world is so hospitable to me, that being a gay man is fashionable, an outrage. Accepting lock, stock, and barrel the fantasies of nineteenth-century doctors and the repressive practices of modern capitalist society looks to me far more like conforming to the world. But there are greater outrages hidden in this argument.

This brings me to my second suspicion about the church, which explains why it is willing to accommodate itself to the mind of the age, to compromise with bourgeois culture: it hopes to maintain its authority and thus its institutional power in society by preventing lesbians and gay men from speaking about their own experiences (this is also the experience of women in the church). The institution benefits, in a material though not a spiritual sense, from a theology that permits it to hand down decisions without any data even being collected, let alone examined.

Love and Romance

In the life and teaching of Jesus, we see that loving human relations take priority over everything else. Jesus healed on the Sabbath. In contrast, the institutional church has accepted the doctrine of bourgeois society that love, like any other commodity, must be handled with thrift. It may occasionally be invested, but on no account is it ever to be given away free.

I distinguish here between love and romance. Carter Heyward points out the difference: "Love is justice. It is not necessarily a happy feeling or a romantic attachment. Love is a way of being in the world."[6] Romance, Hollywood's stock in trade, is everywhere, but it is too self-absorbed to bear any resemblance to what Jesus was talking about. It is a way of getting out of the world.

In theological discussions about love, it is usual to make a distinction between eros and agape. The distinction is based on interpretations of these two Greek words, which, by the nature of language, denote a distinction in Greek culture. Historian John Boswell argues that this distinction was not always carefully drawn even then.[7] While the distinction is not without continuing theological significance, for our purposes it is irrelevant.[8] This is because the distinction bears no relation to the way our cultural patterns assign meanings to gender or sexual practice. What our theological language needs instead is a way to talk about the difference between love and romance.

One reason we have not made a clear theological distinction between the two is that we would have to look at sex (the old distinction, between eros and agape, evades this requirement by assigning all sexuality to eros and all spiritual values to agape). More, it requires us to regard sexual pleasure as a good gift from a generous God. Because the ground of our oppression is our sexual practice, gay men have a contribution to make to this theological task.

The task will not be an easy one. It is commonplace to say that Catholics are repressed about sex. All of us have told jokes about parochial school dances and patent-leather shoes. In fact, I believe that Catholic tradition—in practice and, from time to time, in doctrine as well—has been more sex-positive than other tendencies in Christianity. U.S. Catholics have lost touch with this tradition through a particular set of historical circumstances that would require another book to clarify. For my purposes, two points must suffice.

The first is obvious if often overlooked: Catholic culture is not unitary. This should not surprise us, given the root meaning of the word "catholic." Traditional Catholic cultures have varied in their attitudes toward sexualities. Some Catholic societies were relaxed enough in practice about male-to-male sex to have become refuges for men fleeing more repressive Protestant societies. This sexual economy operated within the Catholic world too. Frenchmen before the revolution used to call homosexual behavior "the Italian vice," and then repair to Italy when they were caught at it.

There are other reasons why rich Englishmen and Germans might have found poor Italians amenable to their blandishments—sexual colonialism, like other kinds, has a long if little-explored history—but the fact remains that poor Englishmen and Germans apparently were not so pliable. George Chauncey tells us that Catholic immigrants, both Italian and Irish, brought this pliability with them to New York; at the same time he cautions us that this did not extend indiscriminately to all sexual acts. In the working-class culture of turn-of-the-century New York, gender conformity, not sexual object choice, controlled men's willingness to participate in homosexual activity.[9] For his part, literary historian Louis Crompton points out that in England, anti-homosexualism, xenophobia and anti-Catholicism were strongly linked in political rhetoric. Trying to explain why executions for sodomy were so prevalent in England during the early nineteenth century while other countries were decriminalizing it, Crompton suggests that "English xenophobia intensified English feelings about sodomy [through] its peculiar connection with English Protestantism. The national tendency to what may be called moral chauvinism [we have inherited this in the United States] had been greatly intensified by the Reformation: the temptation to reaffirm the traditional association of sodomy with Italy was too powerful for Protestant polemicists to resist."[10] He goes on to quote a number of eighteenth-century examples of this rhetoric.

Catholic cultures, with their varied outlooks on sex and especially on homosex, have been transplanted to North America at different times and with different effects. The Spanish Catholicism of New Mexico bears little relation to the Irish Catholicism of Boston. But the general trend has been to try to create a uniform Catholic subculture, especially through the parochial school system. In this process, certain ethnic groups have had more power than others. For the most part, what we may call North Atlantic Catholicism has won out over what we may call Mediterranean Catholicism.

This unifying tendency results from the particular historical position of Catholics in this country, which brings us to the second point. The United States is the political successor to a group of English colonies where Catholicism was persecuted. The Louisiana

Purchase, Irish immigration, and the conquest of northern Mexico had the cumulative effect of increasing the proportion of Catholics to Protestants among U.S. citizens, and thus of strengthening traditional anti-Catholic tendencies in U.S. politics. Anti-Catholic political parties were also mainly middle-class, while most Catholics were working-class.

At that time, concern about sexual practices was growing among the bourgeoisie, part of the construction of respectability as the measure of middle-class status. As a result of this conjunction of middle-class fears, anti-Catholic propaganda was full of passages of forbidden sex. A notorious example was the best-seller of the late 1830s, *Awful Disclosures of the Hôtel Dieu Nunnery,* by Maria Monk, who falsely claimed to be a refugee from that Montreal establishment. Historian Richard Hofstadter offers a pungent explanation of the popularity of this genre: "Anti-Catholicism has always been the pornography of the Puritan."[11] (Around the same time, New Orleans was becoming a favorite destination for the sex tourist, especially men in search of other men.) Such pressures led the Catholic Church's hierarchy, dominated by priests and prelates who had experienced much the same hostility at the hands of the English in Ireland, to take a severely censorious tone toward any sexual practice that was out of accord with the narrow norms of the new bourgeois respectability.

Nothing has changed in the century and a half since. If it had, this book might not be necessary. I introduce this history only to point out that the Roman Catholic Church in the United States adopted its contemporary antisex and thus antigay stance at least in part to deal with a specific set of recent political pressures. We live in a different century now, under a different set of power relations. Our theological tasks are correspondingly different.

With this understanding of the U.S. church's history and tradition with regard to sexual relations, we can now look again at the role of romance in weakening the centrality of love. Romance is love turned inward, in order to make an individual feel better. If requited, it may have this effect on as many as two individuals. Its end is nest building, the creation of a bourgeois family.

Romance does not require sexual consummation. In our society, which cannot accept sex on its own terms, romance is a substitute, almost, one may say, an imitation. Like all imitations, it calls up the original. Romance has become a kind of pornography, geared like pornography toward pleasure without consequences. Like pornography, too, it carries the message that the other person exists to fulfill my own requirements; hence the romantic assumption, carried over into bourgeois marriage, that one can and should change the other to conform to one's own requirements.

This is congruent with the basic measure of value in bourgeois commerce, "What's in it for me?" This question underlies not only romance but philanthropy, that other bourgeois perversion of Christian love. It may help in understanding the distinction I am making to think about the difference between radical work for social change and what we have come to mean by charity. The basic assumption of charity, like romance, is that I have a right and obligation to "fix" people. In philanthropic terms, this has meant turning the poor into simulacra of middle-class reformers, generally without giving the material basis to become the real thing. By contrast, movements such as the Catholic Worker movement have aimed to change the social structure. The difference is well expressed in the description the poet W. H. Auden is supposed to have given of the Worker's constituents: "the *un*deserving poor."

Theologian Monika Hellwig draws a clear picture of the contrast between romance, with its expectations and conventions, and evangelical love: "The Gospels introduce Jesus as one who entered into immediate, shockingly unconventional relationships with people, not evading the human encounter by the choreography of the socio-cultural role definitions."[12] A few examples will illustrate what Hellwig is talking about.

Loosing the Tongue of the Voiceless

John 4:4–43

In the Gospel according to John, we find the story about the woman at the well—significantly, a Samaritan woman. Jesus was on his way back to Galilee after visiting John the Baptist. His journey brought him to Samaria. He was tired and sat down at Jacob's well.

> It was about noon. A Samaritan woman came to draw water, and Jesus said to her, "Give me a drink." (His disciples had gone to the city to buy food.) The Samaritan woman said to him, "How is it that you, a Jew, ask a drink of me, a woman of Samaria?" (Jews did not share things in common with Samaritans.) Jesus answered her, "If you knew the gift of God, and who it is that is saying to you, 'Give me a drink,' you would have asked him, and he would have given you living water." The woman said to him, "Sir, you have no bucket, and the well is deep." (John 4:6–11)

There is something delightful in the contrast between Jesus'
poetic language as reported by John and this woman's extreme
practicality. It seems to carry a subliminal message of the difference
between conventional learning and true knowledge, which in the
Gospels is associated with common folks. In any case the woman
continues:

> "Where do you get that living water? Are you greater than our ancestor
> Jacob, who gave us the well, and with his sons and his flocks drank from
> it?" Jesus said to her, "Everyone who drinks of this water will be thirsty
> again, but those who drink of the water that I will give them will never
> be thirsty. The water that I will give will become in them a spring of
> water gushing up to eternal life." The woman said to him, "Sir, give me
> this water, so that I may never be thirsty or have to keep coming here to
> draw water."
>
> Jesus said to her, "Go, call your husband, and come back." The
> woman answered him, "I have no husband." Jesus said to her, "You are
> right in saying, 'I have no husband'; for you have had five husbands, and
> the one you have now is not your husband. What you have said is true!"
> The woman said to him, "Sir, I see that you are a prophet." (John
> 4:11–19)

Having decided Jesus was a prophet, she asked him some theological questions about the proper form of worship. The discussion
reminds us of the issues in the Jewish–Samaritan split and thus of the
fact that good Jews considered Samaritans heretics, as we saw when
we considered the parable of the good Samaritan.

Then the disciples returned and were surprised to find Jesus
speaking with this woman, this heretic. "But no one said, 'What do
you want?' or, 'Why are you speaking with her?' Then the woman
left her water jar and went back to the city" (4:27–28). She told
everybody about this person who knew everything about her and
so must be the Messiah.

Notice that the story does not end with the expected "Go and
sin no more." Although we are apt to think of this passage as being
about promiscuity, it is not. Jesus does go on to speak with his
disciples about reapers and sowers but not to warn them that she or
they will reap what they sow—the kind of false doctrine so many
preachers use to explain AIDS. Jesus explicitly tells them the
opposite, in fact: "I sent you to reap that for which you did not
labor" (4:38). He never tells the woman that she should leave the
man she is now living with. Jesus is well aware that a woman living
without a man would be an outcast, assumed to be a prostitute. He
has no intention of increasing the suffering of her life by trying to

make her like respectable people. Jesus is no welfare caseworker; he respects the choices she has had to make, recognizing that she must make them in a patriarchal society where she occupies a position of relative powerlessness. His goal is to transform an unjust society, not to "fix" those who suffer injustice so that the existing social order may run more smoothly.

Jesus has not brought up the woman's life as a rebuke. He is not interested in telling her what kind of person she is; she knows her situation better than he. The conversation reveals what kind of person Jesus is. Instead of purveying moral maxims to heretics and sinners, he "enters into shockingly unconventional relationships" with them. His remark about the men in her life is a way of opening a dialogue with her, not of exerting his power over her or of performing a magic trick to prove he is the Messiah. It demonstrates the point of his teaching: don't focus on rituals or worry about which mountain to perform them on, enter the lives of the people you meet.

The Samaritan woman understands the conversation. She does not ask forgiveness for her choices. She asks a theological question. This is a second and equally important point about this story: far from being about promiscuity, it is about who is capable of doing theology. A woman who is a heretic and, in the eyes of a patriarchal community, a sinner grasps the point right away. Her understanding flows out of the same practical good sense that prompted both of her previous questions, "How can I lighten my load of back-breaking daily work by finding a more efficient way of getting water?" and "How do you expect to get water out of a well without a bucket?"

The disciples, as is so often the case, take a little longer to figure things out. They tell Jesus to eat and, when he declines, start debating why. Once again, the religious professionals miss the point.

Luke 10

Another story about who is qualified to do theology comes from Luke 10, immediately following the Good Samaritan story.

[Jesus] entered a certain village, where a woman named Martha welcomed him into her home. She had a sister named Mary, who sat at the Lord's feet and listened to what he was saying. But Martha was distracted by her many tasks; so she came to him and asked, "Lord, do you not care that my sister has left me to do all the work by myself? Tell her then to help me." But the Lord answered her, "Martha, Martha, you are worried and distracted by many things; there is need of only one thing. Mary has chosen the better part, which will not be taken away from her." (Luke 10:38–42)

This story does not sit right with activists. We cannot help feeling that Jesus has been unfair to Martha. But there is an important truth in it. The standard by which Jesus judges is not the bourgeois standard of productivity.

The distinction here is between evangelical love and philanthropy, which is the social version of the distinction between evangelical love and romance. The work of hospitality is important; but in the final reckoning, Jesus asks us not how many homeless people we have fed and sheltered but whether we are willing to sit down and share their company. That is a deeper sign of love than how much food you put on the table.

This is a hard saying for those of us who have certain ingrained ideas about hospitality, such as the one that I got from my good Mississippi Presbyterian mother. We are inclined to think that if people can stand up without assistance after eating supper, we have not given them enough to eat. By his word and example in the house at Bethany, Jesus asks us instead to sit with one another, listen to one another, express our connectedness by sharing time instead of by doing favors. Again, we are asked to enter the lives of those we meet. Only then can we do theology.

There is another level to this: whom we sit with. According to the rules of respectable behavior in Jesus' culture, a male guest sat down with the men. The women were out in the kitchen, and certainly no woman would presume to join their conversation. They certainly would not expect to be commended for doing so. This encounter breaks the rules about socializing between men and women, as well as those about women as theologians.

There is something about this shockingly unconventional relationship that is different from the one Jesus has with the Samaritan woman. Both in the realm of hospitality and in the realm of theology, Mary should be invisible. Jesus makes her visible. In a sense, this is a coming-out story. Mary comes out of the seclusion expected of her, comes out of the closet that respectability has assigned her.

Luke 16:19–31

One of Jesus' best-known parables also shows someone coming out from invisibility to personhood.

There was a rich man who was dressed in purple and fine linen and who feasted sumptuously every day. And at his gate lay a poor man named Lazarus, covered with sores, who longed to satisfy his hunger with what fell from the rich man's table; even the dogs would come and lick his sores. The poor man died and was carried away by the angels to be with Abraham. The rich man also died and was buried. In Hades, where he was being tormented, he looked up and saw Abraham far away with Lazarus by his side. He called out, "Father Abraham, have mercy on me, and send Lazarus to dip the tip of his finger in water and cool my tongue; for I am in agony in these flames." But Abraham said, "Child, remember that during your lifetime you received your good things, and Lazarus in like manner evil things; but now he is comforted here, and you are in agony. Besides all this, between you and us a great chasm has been fixed, so that those who might want to pass from here to you cannot do so, and no one can cross from there to us." He said, "Then, father, I beg you to send him to my father's house—for I have five brothers—that he may warn them, so that they will not also come into this place of torment." Abraham replied, "They have Moses and the prophets; they should listen to them." He said, "No, father Abraham; but if someone goes to them from the dead, they will repent." He said to him, "If they do not listen to Moses and the prophets, neither will they be convinced even if someone rises from the dead." (Luke 16:19–31)

This story, in the way of parables, teaches about love in action by way of its opposite, indifference. The indifference of the rich man makes the beggar at his door invisible. Invisibility, as I said, is one of the basic experiences of lesbians and gay men in our society. The rich man is an example not only of how the materially wealthy in our society often behave but also of how people who think of themselves as spiritually wealthy often behave. Many people who are easily moved by the plight of the poor in Latin America are unable to see the injustice sitting like Lazarus at their own gate.

North Americans have a tendency to try to get our spiritual wealth, like our material goods, on the cheap. We content ourselves with being concerned about oppression set at a safe distance, while ignoring that in which we are more intimate accomplices. Like the rich man asking Lazarus to warn his brothers, we expect the oppressed to do our work for us. Spiritual wealth, like material prosperity, can be the fruit of exploitation. And like material prosperity, it can be a buffer, a way to avoid facing our own homophobia.

I use the word "our" deliberately, because lesbians and gay men grow up in the same heterosexist society as everyone else and cannot help learning much that it teaches. More than that, the oppressed not only are acted on, we also act. Who we are is the result of historic processes in which we play a part. As Sheila Rowbotham, the British Marxist feminist, has pointed out, "Oppression is not an abstract moral condition but a social and historical experience. Its forms and expression change as the mode of production and the relationships between men and women, men and men, women and women, change in society."[13]

Many radical Christians have been unable to hear the cry of lesbians and gay men at the church door. Unlike the institutional churches, this is not because they have an interest in maintaining the existing power arrangements. But indifference can lead them to prefer silence too. Yet until they hear our voices, they will never be free. They will never be raised from the dead.

Learning My Name

It is easy to point fingers. But I must also ask myself what my task is. What have I left undone, not only because of material comfort but because of a spiritual complacency fed both by dwelling on my chosen victimhood and by constantly recounting others' failings? Only I, after all, can free myself from such slave's habits.

Somewhere between the Red Sea and Jordan, we must throw away our hair shirts. To do so, we must name ourselves. We cannot expect the spiritually wealthy to hear our cry through the noise of their revelry. The conventional messengers, "Moses and the prophets," have not done the job. We have to do our part, and the first step is knowing who we are and what we are talking about. We must name ourselves and name our oppression. Naming is how scripture represents people as claiming their own lives and power. A classic example is the story of Jacob at Peniel (Gen. 32:22–32).

Consider Jacob for a minute. This great hero became the ancestor of Israel by cheating twice. First, he cheated his brother Esau out of his inheritance and their father's blessing (Genesis 27). Then he cheated his father-in-law, Laban, out of a flock of sheep, the means of production (Genesis 30–31). (One might think of Jacob as a biblical model of a successful capitalist.) He had learned to live with lies, just as many of us queer folk have had to lie to survive.

But eventually the lies caught up with him. In Genesis 32, Jacob learns his brother Esau (who has always tried to do the right thing) is coming to meet him. Jacob was terrified. He tried flattery, he tried bribes, but nothing made him feel secure. So in the middle of the night, he sent his two wives and his children and all his goods across the Jabbok River.

> Jacob was left alone; and a man wrestled with him until daybreak. When the man saw that he did not prevail against Jacob, he struck him on the hip socket and Jacob's hip was put out of joint as he wrestled with him. Then he said, "Let me go, for the day is breaking." But Jacob said, "I will not let you go, unless you bless me." So he said to him, "What is your name?" And he said, "Jacob." Then the man said, "You shall no longer be called Jacob, but Israel ['the one who strives with God'], for you have striven with God and with humans, and have prevailed." Then Jacob asked him, "Please tell me your name." But he said, "Why is it that you ask my name?" And there he blessed him. (Gen. 32:24–29)

This story has strong similarities to Moses' discussion with the voice in the burning bush. Remember, it was knowing the name of God that gave Moses power to lead God's people to freedom.

The power of naming is emphasized in the next sentence, Gen. 32:30, which concludes the encounter: "So Jacob called the place Peniel ['the face of God'], saying, 'For I have seen God face to face, and yet my life is preserved.' " And then the sun rose. How did Jacob know that his wrestling partner was divine? Because he would not tell Jacob his name.

This is one of my favorite stories, because every time I read it I see something new. There are two parts to the action: the wrestling and the naming. Wrestling must also precede naming in the experience of the oppressed. We learn to name our oppression by struggling with it.

We must also be prepared to get hurt in the process. It does us no good to expect liberation out of the goodness of the oppressors' hearts or to hope that the process will be painless. As Rowbotham notes, "We have to make ourselves not as a projected abstract ideal, but out of the shapes of the here and now."[14] In other words, we have to be practical about the nature of oppression and realistic about its effects. This is why the strategy of putting forward only "acceptable" images of ourselves is doomed to failure. It is a waste of time to complain about how others manage to find the least flattering among us to fill their propaganda. We should be forthright about who we are, not try to pass ourselves off as uniformly loving, wonderful, sweet victims. If we have suffered, we naturally show the marks. Jacob is the ancestor of God's people not because he is perfect but because even though he is terrified, he wrestles with God in a desperate moment.

We must speak with our own voices, in all their imperfection, when responding to God's overtures. Moses stuttered; Israel limped. What matters is not image but integrity. If God calls, we must know who answers. We answer to our true names, because those are the names God calls us by. The cost of learning them is a wrestling match with the divine.

Personal power derives first from coming out, from demonstrating a measure of self-respect. If we have no name or only one we cannot recognize, we are stranded, as Jacob was at the Jabbok River. Canadian writer and activist Gary Kinsman writes of the value to our emerging identity of even the negative medical books of the late nineteenth century: "On the one hand, the perversions are named so that they can be identified and contained. On the other hand, the very naming of the perversions provides the opportunity for people to develop resistance to sexual rule."[15] We recall the earlier importance of renaming ourselves "homosexuals," as K. M. Kertbeny did, or "Uranians," as Ulrichs did, as a way of resisting laws that punished us under the oppressors' names. The historian Allan Bérubé has demonstrated that one way World War II helped spark the gay and lesbian movement in the United States was the consciousness we got from the classification system put in place during the mobilization.[16] I believe that one of the sources of power for the gay liberation movement after Stonewall was that it taught us our own name.

In coming out, we name ourselves to ourselves, so that we can know whom God is calling when the wrestler comes. God then names us to others; that is how Jacob got power.

But are words enough? Can we stop with naming? Coming out is a necessary condition for our liberation, but is it a sufficient condition? The only historical data we have to answer this question come from Germany between the World Wars. Queer social life and political strategies back then show significant points of similarity to ours now, especially the commercialism and the expectation that government action would produce change. English artists such as Christopher Isherwood looked at the scene with envy and hope. But in the end, this coming out only made it easier for the Nazis to round up lesbians and gay men for the concentration camps: easier to identify them and easier to justify punishing them.

This historical precedent suggests that unless our public visibility is accompanied by wrestling with the allocation of social power, especially by building solidarity with other oppressed groups, our movement may be hanging itself out to dry. (I look at solidarity in chapter 5.) It is inadequate to say that Nazism was a uniquely irresistible and ruthless political force to which the rules of political strategy cannot apply, because political exceptions to its force did occur. For example, the "German" wives of a group of Jewish intellectuals were able, nonviolently, to prevent their husbands from being deported from Berlin to the death camps, by means of a resolute and courageous marshaling of what political power they could claim by being "Aryans," women and mothers, and residents of the capital.

They could not have done this as individuals. Coming out, to have a political effect, must have a collective dimension. It must join lesbians and gay men with one another and with others who are oppressed by our social system. This cannot happen, though, unless we have a way of recognizing one another and of conceiving a collective identity. We must name ourselves not only as individuals but as a social group. Then, individually and together, we can, to reiterate Hellwig's phrases, enter into "shockingly unconventional relationships," as we have seen Jesus do, and refuse to evade "the human encounter by the choreography of the socio–cultural role definitions." We are formed within a society that regards the individual as the basic social unit, not the patriarchal household or the clan or the tribe. So we cannot follow Jesus' example unless we know our own names, unless we are comfortable with ourselves as individuals and can reach out from a secure center of personal identity. This is as true of groups as of individuals; lesbians and gay men, in order to build solidarity with other oppressed peoples, have to develop a sense of class consciousness. We look at what that involves next.

CHAPTER 3

In the Image of God

What if Christians believe that the desire of God is that all human beings—not just one—be Christ-bearers? What if we believe that the Love that (as Dante said) "moves the sun and the earth and the stars" deeply yearns for intimate union with every person, desiring that each one participate in the redemption of the world?

—James Nelson, *Between Two Gardens*

Is coming out enough for liberation? Clearly not. Liberation is not a matter of what we know or who we are but what we do with who we are and what we know—our practice.

More concretely, lesbians and gay men are powerless in a specific way: our identities can be nullified. The naming I described in chapter 2 is not irreversible or permanent. It can be repressed; it can be undone. We can undo it ourselves. One way this happens is through the silence that surrounds us. Amid that silence, we sometimes wonder if our oppression is all in our heads. Another way is by accepting the heterosexual assumption, which I discussed earlier.

We can nullify our own acts of naming, too, by subsiding into silence, going back into hiding. Indeed, most of us move back and forth between wrestling, naming, and inaction stemming from uncertainty or helplessness. We know there will be times, shorter or longer, temporary or permanent, when we cannot endure the hatred or indifference we face when we are open.

Thus, one of the deepest shadows on our lives as lesbians and gay men is the fear of annihilation through the erasure of our identities.

Our powerlessness is increased when we are pressured to restrict our struggle to the private sphere. The pressure comes from, in the case of the church, its legitimation of rugged individualism, which echoes society's doctrine that we are all on our own. This cultural doctrine is in direct opposition to the traditional Christian teaching that we are all members of one body of Christ, incorporated into the body through baptism. It is another way in which Christianity has chosen, as Paul put it, to "be conformed to this world." The conformity is hidden, as always, behind a religious mask—in this case, by reducing the image of God in which we are made to its individual aspect, instead of holding up an image of God that also can be seen in community. The God in whose image we are made is the Trinity, but we refuse to recognize this God as long as we do not recognize the social dimension of God's image.

The Creation Stories

If we search the scriptures, we find many passages that present us with such a communal image of God. We may as well begin at the beginning, in the two creation stories of Genesis, where the idea of human beings as the image of God is first expressed.

Genesis 1 follows the sequence of creation through seven days. As the week comes to a close, we read, in vv. 26–28:

> Then God said, "Let us make humankind [*adam*] in our image, according to our likeness; and let them have dominion over the fish of the sea, and over the birds of the air, and over the cattle, and over all the wild animals of the earth, and over every creeping thing that creeps upon the earth." So God created humankind [*ha-adam*] in [God's] image, in the image of God [God] created them; male and female [God] created them. God blessed them, and God said to them, "Be fruitful and multiply, and fill the earth and subdue it; and have dominion over the fish of the sea and over the birds of the air and over every living thing that moves upon the earth."

In this story, the divine image from the outset has two parts, the male and the female. Genesis does not say that God created "images" but, rather, in God's image a single species with male and female varieties. God's image is richer than the individual natures we each claim in ourselves; it is a collective divine image. We are created in community.

Nor are we told specifically that procreation is the function of this image of God. "God blessed them," we are told, "and God said to them, 'Be fruitful and multiply.'" The second part is the substance of the blessing, the means of carrying out the charge that follows. The function is stewardship of creation. This "image of God" is not created for reproduction as an end in itself but for stewardship. The blessing is a sign of God's love, to be found in this paired image, a sign of God's desire for more lovers to work together.

This creation story seems not to have conveyed all that the compilers of Genesis thought needed saying, however. It did not tell enough about God's purpose in creation or about the nature of human beings as we were created. So the compilers included a second creation story, which begins a few verses into Genesis 2. Here we learn about how God "planted a garden in Eden, in the east." This garden was intended as a dwelling for a pair of humans, whose creation took place in two stages, rather than in a single act of creation as in Genesis 1. The sovereign God formed *ha-adam* "from the dust of the ground [*min ha-adamah*], and breathed into [its] nostrils the breath of life; and [*ha-adam*] became a living being" (2:7).

This being, or as the Hebrew literally describes it, this living soul, God placed in the garden, again as a steward. After giving this steward instructions, the sovereign God said, " 'It is not good that [*ha-adam*] should be alone. I will make . . . a helper as [a] partner" (2:18). God put the human being to sleep and took out a rib and made a woman. At this point, not before, the text uses the words *ish* and *ishshah,* man and woman.

Again, notice what we are told and not told. God does not say, "I need to find some way for this human being to procreate." The woman is not created to be a mother but to be a partner. "There-fore"—because two beings were created out of one—"a man leaves his father and his mother and clings to his wife, and they become one flesh" (2:24). It is "not good," God thinks, for the human being to be alone. The image of God is unsatisfactory, incomplete, as long as there is only one kind of human being.

In fact, this second story bears a striking resemblance to the one Plato tells in his *Symposium.* That story describes us as half-beings, formed out of primeval whole beings; ever since, we have been searching for our other halves. This story is meant as an explanation of sexual attraction, but in the Athenian context, it serves also to explain why some people search for a member of the other sex and some a member of the same: it depends on what kind of primeval whole they were split from.

In respect to Genesis as it has come down to us, we ought to read these two stories not as separate and self-contained but as somehow making up a single creation myth. Taken in its parts, this myth teaches about a human species that is collectively an image of God (Genesis 1), in need of companionship and variety (Genesis 2), and always attracted sexually to other human beings. It claims to explain why human beings come in two varieties and to use that to explain sexual attraction. It makes no particular claim that sexual attraction comes in only one form—that is not what the story is about—just that it is part and parcel of our created nature. (It follows, though I do not propose to take that up here, that sexual attraction is not simply a result of the Fall.)

Taken as a whole, the creation myth tells us that people need one another in order to become the image of God, to become fully human.

Trinity, Not Heterosexuality

Fundamentalists and their fellow travelers often use these creation stories to prove that "homosexuality" is unnatural. If, as I have argued, our contemporary notion of homosexuality as a condition is the result of medical notions of naturalness no older than the nineteenth century, this is using scripture in an intellectually shoddy way. But then, the same people also cite these stories to prove that women are required to be submissive to their fathers and husbands within the patriarchal structure of the nineteenth-century family, which the same scientists claimed embodied "natural" maleness and femaleness. Ironically, fundamentalism arose precisely to defend Christianity against that kind of science.

The lesbian theologian Sally Gearhart, herself a product of this subculture, gives a powerful account of the social effects of the fundamentalist way of reading Genesis in an essay in which she goes on to challenge her roots. She begins by describing the world she sees, as any liberation theologian does:

> Exclusive heterosexuality has to be understood as a perversion of [humanity's] natural state. We very quickly rob infants of their health and wholesomeness. We require them from birth to fall into one of two widely differing and oppositely valued categories: girls and boys. We further require them to obliterate half their loving nature so as to become lovers *only* of a member of the opposite sex. It is as if at birth without our knowledge or consent we are injected with a heavy addictive drug that will assure our limitation to one sex role and to exclusively heterosexual relations. We're hooked early. We're hetero-

sexual junkies. When we become adults, we push that drug ourselves, not just on the adults and children but on every newborn infant. To kick the habit is near impossible.[1]

Gearhart then goes back to scripture, to Genesis, and looks at it more closely in the light of her suspicion. She comes up with a new understanding of these stories, one that is in stark contrast with the foregoing: "An accurate translation of the Hebrew word for god (Elohim) in the first Genesis narrative (1:27) posits her/him as an androgynous (a gynandrous) being, having both sexes complete within her/him."[2] (The grammatical number of the noun *elohim* is plural.)

Here Gearhart is in solidly orthodox company. In classic Christian theology, the doctrine of the Trinity underlies the act of creation. God is one but with three persons or aspects. Mystical tradition understands this as a way of conveying the fact that love, which is God's essential nature, must find expression in relation. Thus, each aspect of God requires a continual exchange of love with the other persons of the Trinity. In the fullness of time, this continual outpouring of love overflows in creation. God creates us out of a need for more lovers.

It follows that the blessing "Be fruitful and multiply" (Gen. 1:22, 28) is an extension of this creative energy, part of the way we are in the image of the Trinity. It is, perhaps, a way of speaking of love as always multiplying, moving from couples to groups. This is, of course, a very different understanding of love from the one endorsed in bourgeois society, which is concerned with limiting the expression of love to a few approved patterns. To connect this to the situation of lesbians and gay men, I return to Gearhart:

> In this light, it is not the Lesbian or the Gay man who is "unnatural" but rather the heterosexual person. The Gay relationship moves toward expression not because it is conditioned from birth to do so or because it is approved of by society or because it is given any positive reinforcement whatsoever. Clearly the opposite is true. The motivating energy of the Gay relationship flows rather from inside the persons themselves, from sources that are far more authentic than are responses to external programming.[3]

This is a radical departure from the usual understanding of the creation myth. It may be helpful to put it alongside several other stories.

No Private Salvation: Moses, Esther, Rahab

Moses

When I discussed Exodus in chapter 1, it was to note how one community was marked for liberation. I want to look now at Moses himself. We can think of the early part of the story of Moses, up to his return to Egypt in obedience to the commission from the burning bush, as Moses' coming out.

Moses, a Hebrew by birth, was put in the care of pharaoh's daughter and brought up as an Egyptian. As a result of his upbringing, Moses identified not with the Hebrew people but with the oppressor, the Egyptians. He surely knew his true identity, for his natural mother was taken on by pharaoh's daughter as his nurse. But Moses kept this self-knowledge secret: remember how, when Moses killed the overseer, he looked first to one side, then to the other. Let us go back to that story in Exodus 2.

"The next day," we read in Ex. 2:13, Moses "saw two Hebrews fighting; and he said to the one who was in the wrong, 'Why do you strike your fellow Hebrew?' " Notice Moses' careful choice of words: *your* fellow Hebrew. But it did not work. He got back a retort that suggested his true identity was no secret: " 'Who made you a ruler and judge over us? Do you mean to kill me as you killed the Egyptian?' Then Moses was afraid and thought, 'Surely the thing is known.' " (2:14). What thing, exactly? His killing of the overseer, or his being a Hebrew? Whichever we choose, the consequences are serious:

> When Pharaoh heard of it, he sought to kill Moses.
> But Moses fled from Pharaoh. He settled in the land of Midian, and sat down by a well. The priest of Midian had seven daughters. They came to draw water, and filled the troughs to water their father's flock. But some shepherds came and drove them away. Moses got up and came to their defense and watered their flock. When they returned to their father Reuel, he said, "How is it that you have come back so soon today?" They said, "An Egyptian helped us against the shepherds." (Ex. 2:15–19)

Notice that Moses has continued to pass as an Egyptian. Presumably he was identified as such by his clothes and language.

> [Reuel] said to his daughters, "Where is he? Why did you leave the man? Invite him to break bread." Moses agreed to stay with the man,

and he gave Moses his daughter Zipporah in marriage. She bore a son, and he named him Gershom; for he said, "I have been an alien [ger] residing in a foreign land." (Ex. 2:20–22)

Then Moses went out one day with his flock, saw the miraculous bush that burned and yet was not consumed, and was charged with a mission, one he was not particularly willing to accept. "Moses said to the LORD, 'O my Lord, I have never been eloquent, neither in the past nor even now that you have spoken to your servant; but I am slow of speech and slow of tongue' " (4:10). God and Moses argued the point for a while, Moses asking God to send someone else. Finally,

the anger of the LORD was kindled against Moses and he said, 'What of your brother Aaron, the Levite? I know that he can speak fluently; even now he is coming out to meet you, and when he sees you his heart will be glad. You shall speak to him and put the words in his mouth; and I will be with your mouth and with his mouth, and will teach you what you shall do.' " (Ex. 4:14–15)

Moses got his father-in-law's permission to return to Egypt with his wife and children. Along the way, a curious incident took place:

On the way, at a place where they spent the night, the LORD met him and tried to kill him. But Zipporah took a flint and cut off her son's foreskin, and touched Moses' feet with it, and said, "Truly you are a bridegroom of blood to me!" So [God] let him alone. It was then she said, "A bridegroom of blood by circumcision." (Ex. 4:24–26)

What is this all about? Moses, apparently, was so intent on passing that he omitted to circumcise his son as the law required. He was still trying to assimilate, to live according to the customs of those around him. He wanted to be considered an Egyptian, even though he had seen how the Egyptians treated Hebrew slaves and had been so outraged by it that he killed someone. Perhaps, indeed, that is why he tried to assimilate, because he felt guilty about killing an Egyptian, one of the people he had been brought to think of as cultured, good, and wise. It is common for colonized people to imitate their oppressors. As we have seen, the freed Hebrew slaves spent forty years in the desert unlearning this habit. Zipporah, fortunately, never had this conditioning. Moses had always been a foreigner to her; it did not really matter what brand. Hebrew or Egyptian, she loved him anyhow.

God, though, expected Moses to live as a Hebrew. God sees our true identities. And, like Zipporah, God loves us anyhow.

Their journey continued; they met Aaron, and the joint ministry began. Even Moses, the great prophet, did not work alone. He was part of a collective. Such sacrifices as doing penance alone in the desert, even to the extent of cutting himself off from all that had been dear to him, in exile from the people he tried to pass among, meant nothing to God. Instead, God sent Moses, newly reincorporated into the people whom God meant to liberate, to work out his own salvation on a political mission.

Esther

Esther is more explicitly a model of solidarity than is Moses. The book of Esther is unusual because God is never named in the original Hebrew version. This has distressed some people, but it is meaningful to those of us who have sometimes suffered at the hands of those who claim to say and do everything in God's name.

Esther is set during the Babylonian captivity, after the conquerors of Jerusalem had deported the royal family, the court officials, the priests and so on to ensure that the political organization had been destroyed. By the time of this story, Babylon, in turn, had been conquered by the Persians.

King Artaxerxes divorced his first queen, Vashti, an uppity woman who refused to dance for him and his guests. He held a kind of beauty pageant to find a new queen, which is where we pick up the story (Esth. 2:5, Greek version, NRSV).[4]

"Now there was a Jew in Susa the capital whose name was Mordecai; . . . he had been taken captive from Jerusalem among those whom King Nebuchadnezzar of Babylon had captured. And he had a foster child . . . and her name was Esther." In the Hebrew version of this tale, we learn of a custom many Jews still follow, that of having two names, a Hebrew name and a name more familiar to the surrounding culture. Hadassah is Esther's Hebrew name, and Esther is her public name. Plainly, by this stage of the captivity many of the deportees were trying to assimilate. (This is the root of the schism with the Samaritans after the deportees were allowed to return.)

> When [Esther's] parents died, [Mordecai] brought her up to womanhood as his own. The girl was beautiful in appearance. So, when the decree of the king was proclaimed, and many girls were gathered in Susa the capital in custody of Gai, Esther also was brought to Gai. . . . Now Esther had not disclosed her people or country, for Mordecai had commanded her not to make it known. And every day Mordecai

walked in the courtyard of the harem, to see what would happen to
Esther. (Esth. 2:7–8, 10–11)

Then we read about the beauty contest. The women who had
been picked out by the advisers went in one by one. In the end,
Esther proved to be the most acceptable to the king and so was
made queen. Meanwhile—like any good novel, this one has several
plots going at once—two of the royal bodyguards were conspiring
to assassinate King Artaxerxes. "The matter became known to
Mordecai, and he warned [Queen] Esther, who in turn revealed the
plot to the king" (2:22), and as a result, Mordecai's star was on the
rise.

But now the plot is thickened by a bit of jockeying for power at
court:

> After these events King Artaxerxes promoted Haman son of Hamme-
> datha, a Bougean, advancing him and granting him precedence over all
> the king's Friends. So all who were at court used to do obeisance to
> Haman, for so the king had commanded to be done. Mordecai,
> however, did not do obeisance. Then the king's courtiers said to
> Mordecai, "Mordecai, why do you disobey the king's command?" Day
> after day they spoke to him, but he would not listen to them. Then they
> informed Haman that Mordecai was resisting the king's command.
> Mordecai had told them that he was a Jew. (Esth. 3:1–4)

In other words, Mordecai bowed to God alone. This is the
struggle of all who belong to minorities: how far to go toward
assimilation. Mordecai made some accommodation to Persian custom, as in the matter of Esther's name, and tried to minimize the
ethnic difference by advising her to pass. But when it came to
central issues, Mordecai did not compromise.

"So when Haman learned that Mordecai was not doing obei-
sance to him, he became furiously angry, and plotted to destroy all
the Jews under Artaxerxes' rule" (3:5–6). Note that the issue is
Mordecai's nationality. For Haman, there is no issue of personal
morality involved, although living in a liberal democracy, we tend
to read this as a tale about religious tolerance. In the cosmopolitan
centers of the ancient world, a degree of religious pluralism was
taken for granted. The local gods rarely claimed universal jurisdic-
tion, and as long as political hierarchies and social proprieties were
respected, migrants from elsewhere were generally free to worship
their traditional deities.

But as far as Haman was concerned, Mordecai no longer respected the hierarchies and proprieties. Haman's prestige and

power were on the line. So, "in the twelfth year of King Artaxerxes Haman came to a decision by casting lots [in Hebrew, *purim*], taking the days and the months one by one, to fix on one day to destroy the whole race of Mordecai. The lot fell on the fourteenth day of the month of Adar" (4:7).

What we have here is a plan for a "final solution." All Jews who would not subordinate their religious practice to the state's requirements were to be destroyed. That Haman's plot is an exception to a general multiculturalism is revealed in the complexities of promulgating the order he secured from the king to carry out his crime. A platoon of royal secretaries was needed to write letters to various satraps and governors and officials of the 127 provinces of Persia, "each in his own language." Of course, the king in whose name this was done did not know, because of Mordecai's strategy of assimilation, that Esther (or Mordecai, for all we know) was one of the people that Haman had permission to destroy.

Esther heard that Mordecai had been protesting this decree in sackcloth and ashes:

> Then Esther summoned Hachratheus, the eunuch who attended her, and ordered him to get accurate information for her from Mordecai . . . [who then] gave him a copy of what had been posted in Susa for their destruction, to show to Esther, and he told him to charge her to go in to the king and plead for his favor in behalf of the people. "Remember," he said, "the days when you were an ordinary person, being brought up under my care—for Haman, who stands next to the king, has spoken against us and demands our death. Call upon the Lord; then speak to the king in our behalf, and save us from death."
>
> Hachratheus went in and told Esther all these things. And she said to him, "Go to Mordecai and say, 'All nations of the empire know that if any man or woman goes to the king inside the inner court without being called, there is no escape for that person. Only the one to whom the king stretches out the golden scepter is safe—and it is now thirty days since I was called to go to the king.' "
>
> . . . Mordecai told [Hachratheus] to go back and say to her, "Esther, do not say to yourself that you alone among all the Jews will escape alive. . . . Who knows whether it was not for such a time as this that you were made queen?" Then Esther gave the messenger this answer to take back to Mordecai: "Go and gather all the Jews who are in Susa and fast on my behalf. . . . After that I will go to the king, contrary to the law, even if I must die." (Esth. 4:5, 8–11, 13–16)

Mordecai prayed; Esther prayed. Then Esther went to the king, "majestically adorned":

> Lifting his face, flushed with splendor, [Artaxerxes] looked at her in fierce anger. The queen faltered, and turned pale and faint, and collapsed on the head of the maid who went in front of her. Then God changed the spirit of the king to gentleness, and in alarm he sprang from his throne and took her in his arms until she came to herself. He comforted her with soothing words, and said to her, "What is it, Esther? I am your husband. Take courage; You shall not die, for our law applies only to our subjects. Come near."
>
> Then he raised the golden scepter and touched her neck with it. (Esth. 15:7–11)

But Esther did not beg for her people yet. The king offered to grant any request. Instead, she invited him to a dinner, along with Haman. They accepted, and after some wine, the king asked her again to name her favor. "She said, 'My petition and request is: if I have found favor in the sight of the king, let the king and Haman come to the dinner that I shall prepare them, and tomorrow I will do as I have done today' "(5:7–8).

At Queen Esther's second banquet, the king yet again promised her any favor she would name. "She answered and said, 'If I have found favor with the king, let my life be granted me at my petition, and my people at my request. For we have been sold, I and my people, to be destroyed' " (7:3–4). The king demanded the name of the one responsible, and she pointed to Haman. The destruction of the Jews was averted.

Mordecai and other Jews at court had tried to assimilate to the culture as much as they could, even taking other names, to avoid drawing attention to their nationality. They admitted to the truth only when strong religious motives forced them and they risked destruction. The effect of their strategy was that one powerful demagogue, Haman, was able to define them as the enemy and order them obliterated.

Esther had the most to lose by revealing herself. Despite Mordecai's needling remark, the chances were good that if she said nothing, she would escape. She had carefully concealed the fact that she was a Jew, and we are given no reason to assume that she would have been included in the massacre. Nevertheless, she confronted the power of the state, which legitimizes destruction of a people under the guise of national security. She could not, in the moment of crisis, continue to hide. She had to publicly become one of her people in order to save them. She had to "come out," so to speak, as a Jew. Her status as queen gave her access to the throne (even that access was limited by law), but that by itself did not give her power.

Only her identification of herself with her people brought enough power to affect the king's decree. Only her identification with the oppressed saved herself and them. Identifying with the oppressed, she manifested the image of the God who liberates. She achieved wholeness, the full measure of the image of God, in proclaiming herself part of a people.

Finally, she found her salvation not as a wife and mother, where no doubt she had been trained as a Jewish woman to look for it. Rather, she was saved because she took political action. True, she was in a unique position to do so: she was the queen. She identified herself with the oppressed, but she did not take the role of helpless victim.

Rahab

Another woman in scripture, who lived at the opposite end of the social scale, saved the people who had wandered in the desert for forty years. We meet her, Rahab, in Josh. 2:1–15:

> Then Joshua son of Nun sent two men secretly from Shittim as spies, saying, "Go, view the land, especially Jericho." So they went, and entered the house of a prostitute whose name was Rahab, and spent the night there. The king of Jericho was told, "Some Israelites have come here tonight to search out the land." So the king of Jericho sent orders to Rahab, "Bring out the men who have come to you, who entered your house, for they have come only to search out the whole land." But the woman took the two men and hid them. Then she said, "True, the men came to me, but I did not know where they came from. And when it was time to close the gate at dark, the men went out. Where the men went I do not know. Pursue them quickly, for you can overtake them." She had, however, brought them up to the roof and hidden them with the stalks of flax that she had laid out on the roof. So the men pursued them on the way to the Jordan as far as the fords. As soon as the pursuers had gone out, the gate was shut.
>
> Before they went to sleep, she came up to them on the roof and said to the men: "I know that the LORD has given you the land, and that dread of you has fallen on us, and that all the inhabitants of the land melt in fear before you. For we have heard how the LORD dried up the water of the Red Sea before you." . . . Then she let them down by a rope through the window, for her house was on the outer side of the city wall and she resided within the wall itself. (Josh. 2:1–15)

Later we learn that she was the only inhabitant of Jericho to survive its capture.

Now Rahab the prostitute is, like Esther the queen, the instrument of God; and she finds her own salvation by acting, by becoming one with God's people, even though they are technically her city's enemies. She is named in the genealogy that opens Matthew as one of the ancestors of Jesus. On two counts she was an unlikely candidate for this honor: she worked in the sex business and she betrayed her fellow citizens. Neither would win her much respect today. But we may argue that the outcast status of her profession allowed her to see beyond the narrow interest of her city to become part of the mighty work of God in history. No doubt, she was an outcast among the respectable people of Jericho. Why should she have indulged in patriotism? Rahab, precisely because she was a sex worker, was open to God. Unlike Queen Esther, she could not rely on her closeness to power to save God's agents. Instead, she relied first on the knowledge that unknown men could come to her house without arousing suspicion and, second, on her wits. Finally, free of "patriotic" attachment to a power structure that scorned her, she was also free to see the path of solidarity with the stranger.

An article by Robert W. Wood, which appeared in *ONE Magazine,* is worth noting here, very briefly. Wood observes that Rahab and Sarah are the only two women in the list of models of faith given in Hebrews 11 and that Rahab and Abraham are the two examples in James 2 of justification by faith.[5]

The Memory of Destruction

The stories of Esther and Rahab remind us of two things. First, these heroines become the image of the liberating God by moving beyond personal identity to solidarity. Second, they do not rely on ordinary power or on the world's prudence; in Paul's words, they do not conform themselves to this world. Rather than rely on the power of the state, whether on Haman or on the king of Jericho, they defy it.

We cannot read the book of Esther without recalling that the destruction Haman prepared for the Jews nearly came to pass within living memory. The events of Purim have become a more somber story in our generation. We should remember that the Jews were not the only people singled out for destruction by the Nazis. Gay men, because they represented a degeneration of German bloodstock, and lesbians, because they were "antisocial" in refusing to bear children to replenish that bloodstock, were chosen as well.[6]

In one respect, the experience of gay men was different from that of any other group. When the Allied forces, whether British or American in the west or Russian in the east, came into the camps, they decided not to release the gay men they found there, on the assumption that they had been properly condemned to these death camps by the law of Germany. No compensation has been awarded to gay Holocaust survivors by the Federal Republic of Germany; nor were any steps taken to repeal the Nazi version of the old Prussian antigay statute until the German Democratic Republic did so in 1968. (The Federal Republic followed suit a year later. So much for the idea that capitalist governments are better for gay men than Marxist ones.)

This is the experience memorialized by the pink triangle and by the black triangle that was the badge of antisocials, which the Nazis forced many lesbians to wear. This recent history echoes in the minds of lesbians and gay men when public figures, in the name of AIDS prevention, call for tattooing HIV positive individuals or quarantining "carriers" in concentration camps. It contributes to gay men's suspicion that some powerful heterosexual interests ignored AIDS in the hope that it would kill off undesirables and spare everyone else. It remains in the fear of personal annihilation through physical violence and often murder, for which all too often the gay-basher and murderer are set free.

This fear of annihilation forces us to stop seeking individual salvation. So great a threat can be met only by working together, not only among lesbians and gay men but with other movements of oppressed people struggling for liberation.

The Worship of Idols

Understanding that we must move beyond personal identity and personal salvation to solidarity is simply a beginning. We have too much experience working in coalitions where our labor is welcome only as long as we stay invisible. We have discussed the virtues of invisibility for those who want to keep us oppressed. On a personal level, invisibility feels like a small, temporary death and thus feeds the fear of annihilation. It is difficult to give our best to any coalition when big chunks of our experience, the raw materials we draw on for our politics, are unmentionable.

Even where we are free to work openly as lesbians and gay men, movements for justice and peace in this country often operate in ways that leave oppressed groups vaguely unsatisfied. For instance, they divide the personal from the political. And their approach is mechanistic, concentrating on the product at the expense of the process. These ways of working assume that a political movement is nothing more than a tool. Most movements are not interested in providing community, emotional support, or any sense of belonging among those who take part. We come together, we do hard political work, we go home. We do not expect our movements to be home, since home in a bourgeois society is a refuge from work. So naturally, people who are parts of these movements burn out and drop away, the movement dwindles, and at the next crisis we have to start all over from scratch.

So it is worth asking ourselves what kind of movement Jesus tried to build. Where did he begin? Matthew 4:18–22 tells one version:

> As [Jesus] walked by the Sea of Galilee, he saw two brothers, Simon, who is called Peter, and Andrew his brother, casting a net into the sea—for they were fishermen. And he said to them, "Follow me, and I will make you fish for people." Immediately they left their nets and followed him. As he went from there, he saw two other brothers, James son of Zebedee and his brother John, in the boat with their father Zebedee, mending their nets, and he called them. Immediately they left the boat and their father, and followed him.

Notice that they drop everything. We know (because Jesus heals Peter's mother-in-law) that Peter is married. There is no mention here of Peter arranging to take care of his family. We are told explicitly that James and John just walk out on their father, to whom presumably they have both business and family obligations. Elsewhere we hear similar advice for other followers of Jesus. In Matt. 8:18–22, we read:

> Now when Jesus saw great crowds around him, he gave orders to go over to the other side. A scribe then approached and said, "Teacher, I will follow you wherever you go." And Jesus said to him, "Foxes have holes, and birds of the air have nests; but the Son of Man has nowhere to lay his head." Another of his disciples said to him, "Lord, first let me go and bury my father." But Jesus said to him, "Follow me, and let the dead bury their own dead."

This is not a movement for family values. It is not built on a husband, a wife, and 2.3 children in the suburbs; nor is it built on the biology-as-destiny orthodoxy that informs recent court decisions in adoption cases. Jesus' movement cut through even the most important relations in society, such as the duty to bury one's father. In Matt. 12:46–50, Jesus himself set the example:

> While he was still speaking to the crowds, his mother and his brothers were standing outside, wanting to speak to him. Someone told him, "Look, your mother and your brothers are standing outside, wanting to speak to you." But to the one who had told him this, Jesus replied, "Who is my mother, and who are my brothers?"

Remember, Matthew is the evangelist who devotes his whole first chapter to "begats," all the way back to Adam, so that we can know precisely who Jesus' mother and brothers were. But here he tells us that Jesus, "pointing to his disciples, . . . said, 'Here are my mother and my brothers! For whoever does the will of my Father in heaven is my brother and sister and mother.' "

The Jesus movement is not a workplace from which we go home to our families for emotional support. It constructs a new family not defined by blood or by marriage. It is the family of hearers and doers of the Word.

For lesbians and gay men, this is good news indeed. Many of us have been thrown out of our families. All of us hear those with power in the church and in the state preach that such bourgeois families are the basic unit of society and the church. This is why they say we must be cast out: we are a threat to the family. But their kind of family, if we believe Matthew, does not seem to be the basic unit of the community that Jesus built. Indeed, it could not be, because such forms of family did not exist in the society where Jesus worked. If we put the bourgeois family at the heart of Jesus' message instead of the assembly of hearers and doers, we worship an idol.

Some will object that we must be prepared to accept the reality of social change in history. They are right. But we must also be able to accept the social changes that have forged new forms of family among lesbians and gay men. Underlying the debate over family values is an assumption that "families" and "lesbians and gay men" are two separate groups, without overlap. In fact, we are all part of the families we grew up in. We may not always get along well with them, but a lot of straight people do not either. Many of us get along fine. Often we are heads of families ourselves, lesbians especially—if they have been allowed to keep their children. The bourgeois family is not necessarily any more foreign to lesbians and gay men than to others. We, too, may be guilty of worshiping that idol.

Framing the debate on the family in terms of an all-or-nothing choice between some well-defined unity unchanged throughout history, on the one hand, and the liberation of lesbians and gay men, on the other, is a kind of shell game. It diverts our attention from the uncertain place of families in a changing society, for good and for ill, and from how a changing society in turn molds families, also for good or for ill. These are issues for theologians along with everyone else, and lesbians and gay men, being, so to speak, both inside and outside the institution, have valuable insights. In this, as in so many aspects of U.S. culture that are so familiar as to be opaque to their beneficiaries, Ethan Mordden, the chronicler of New York gay life in the 1970s and 1980s, aptly observes: "We have to know more than the straights know: have to understand what we are as well as what they are—have to find *our* unique place in *their* culture."[7]

Idols are false gods that we worship because they are easier to manage than the real thing. We have made the bourgeois family into an idol because it, unlike the living God, gives us permission to confine our concern only to our own kin and kind. It tells us it is OK to worry above all about keeping our families safe from the rest of society.

That is precisely the kind of family Jesus tells us to reject.

J. B. Metz, the German political theologian, discusses this in *The Emergent Church*. He writes, "The family [is] the sphere to which the Christian virtues in their privatized form are allocated."[8] This is part of a longer discussion of what Metz calls "bourgeois religion," which, he claims, has privatized Christianity, narrowing how we think about the practice of the Christian life. It is Christianity made safe for capitalism. The family is one place this happens: "Here love is forced into a kind of diminished version of itself, becoming a love that renounces comprehensive justice. But where Christian love is lived nowhere else than in the family, it soon becomes impossible to live it there either."[9]

To understand Metz's point, we need only look at the reasons many "pro-family" conservatives offer for their antigay stance. Many, of course, offer none, regarding the truth of their statements as self-evident, if not divinely inspired. But Midge Decter wrote an article that appeared in the September 1980 issue of *Commentary* that reveals a lot about the function of the bourgeois family in modern capitalist society. Decter and her husband Norman Podhoretz were major voices of the neo-conservative movement of former liberals in the middle 1970s. As board members of the

Committee on the Present Danger, they helped to lay the ground-work for Ronald Reagan's election to the presidency. To summarize very briefly, she argues in the *Commentary* article, "The Boys on the Beach," that open acknowledgment of gay men serves as a mockery and a temptation to straight men, who apparently all regret having married. Why? Because marriage brings with it the obligation to support women, at the expense of men's own "natural" impulse to promiscuity and irresponsibility. This obligation, a vital prop of civilized society, is now under attack by socialists and feminists. Only if forced will men continue to let themselves be trapped into marriage. Openly gay men—in Decter's world, all white and well-to-do—offer straight men a living alternative of permanent adolescence. This is why we are a threat to "family values".[10]

We can also detect in "The Boys on the Beach" a strategy of dismissing "gays"—understood to be exclusively white and male—as neither deserving nor needing any sympathy because they are already well-to-do and privileged. This approach worked in the 1992 campaign to amend Colorado's constitution to invalidate any gay rights legislation.

Decter's article should be read alongside the considerable body of feminist writing about the nineteenth-century "cult of true womanhood." This took hold as the economic system that we now take for granted was being shaped and, we should recall, at the same time as the invention of "the homosexual," in many cases by the same authorities. Since in Decter's description this family structure seems as cruel as any libertine could wish to paint it, one is left perplexed as to how it can be simultaneously praised as the foundation of the freest, fairest, and most generous social system known to human history.

Gay men, then—lesbians are rarely visible in this picture—are a threat to the bourgeois family because we offer a beguiling way out, one that any man would take if he could. This may explain the paradox that homosexuality, as depicted by the same people, is both sickeningly unnatural but fortunately very rare, on the one hand, and so tempting that it must be made unspeakable, on the other.

The family, church leaders say often and loudly, cannot survive the presence of open lesbians and gay men. But the family they worship as a school for Christian love seems doomed to collapse under its contradictions, if we are to believe defenders like Decter. It is based on the exploitation of male labor, in a kind of mirror image of feminist critiques. It is based not on love but on entrap-

ment. Even its promoters seem to have found that Metz's predic-
tion—"where Christian love is lived nowhere else than in the
family, it soon becomes impossible to live it there either"—has
come true.

A New Holy Family

The bourgeois family structure as described above cannot be what
the church has in mind when it preaches the need to revitalize the
family. It is a mystery, therefore, why the church hierarchy should
make common cause with those who call the family the foundation
of society. We can understand why Jesus counseled his followers
not to be caught in a net that would hinder them from moving
beyond the ties of blood obligation to build God's commonwealth.
We, too, would do well to let the dead bury their own dead.

Instead, we should embrace the example of Jesus as "one who
entered into immediate, shockingly unconventional relationships
with people, not evading the human encounter by the choreography
of the socio-cultural role definitions," to recall Monika Hellwig (see
chapter 2). Jesus' example opens the way to a social-change movement that does not neglect our need for community, for mutual aid
and support; but first we have to leave behind the model of family
with which we have lived for the last century and a half.

We also have to leave behind the halfway house many radical
Christians have inhabited. By this I mean the model of family that
clings to hearthside comfort while grafting onto it the practice of
the works of mercy. Vincent de Paul told us to do the works of
mercy in such a way that the poor can forgive us for the bread we
give them. This is why Jesus went to eat with sinners. He offered his
loving company and accepted their love in return. Unless we are
willing to receive it in return, love is turned into something else we
inflict on others. Straight people, on learning I am gay, often assure
me that they "love me anyway." That is sweet of them; I am glad to
hear it; but their reassurance is beside the point. The real test is, will
they let me love them? As theologian Dorothee Soelle notes:

> The concept "love of others" denotes a relationship between people,
> and not the virtue of any single person. Traditionally, this point has
> been reflected in the designation of love for others as a "supernatural"
> or theological virtue. It is self-evident that what is supernatural cannot
> be possessed or acquired by individuals. The supernatural virtues—
> faith, hope and charity—are concepts that describe life itself, that tell us

what it means to live life to the full. They are relational concepts, concepts of connectedness.[11]

Thus, simply loving does not get us off the hook. The power of loving where it is forbidden—the power of extending love across boundaries, the power of offering love where we are not supposed to—is a countersign to the narrow society that forbids such loving. Drawing ever-tighter boundaries around the universe of acceptable recipients of our love is the hallmark of the godless society built in the two hundred years since the Industrial Revolution reordered society toward production. The invention and simultaneous stigmatizing of homosexuality by medicine was a moral enclosure as necessary to the power of capital as the theft of land by physical enclosure of the commons ever was.

Godly love can never be confined to women's space, as nineteenth-century moralists tried to do so that men would be free to go out and exploit others. But love is forbidden to lesbians and gay men even in the domestic sphere. If it flourishes there anyway, in defiance of the rules, the church denounces it as "disordered"! "Ordering" our love cannot be squared with the command to love our sovereign God with all our hearts and all our minds and all our strength. Soelle writes, "May we hope that love which does not solely reside in the family and is not willing to forgo justice has future possibilities that we, at the end of the bourgeois era, are not yet able to perceive."[12]

The Catholic Worker movement is a good model of families open to such a way of love. A classic example is the story of Dorothy and Bill Gauchat. Friends of Dorothy Day and Peter Maurin (the founders of the Catholic Worker movement in the 1930s), they built themselves a farm in Avon, Ohio. Bill worked as a schoolteacher to keep it going. They had children. So far, so good: they had made it to the halfway house.

Then, one day, a county health worker came with a child who had been abandoned by its parents because of a severe birth defect that meant the child would probably not live more than a year. The health worker told the Gauchats, "We have no place to take this child. Can you take care of this child for just a year?" The Gauchats saw no way in conscience to refuse, although they were not sure they could really manage it. Their family expanded then and there, and it expanded again, and again, and again, until there were more than a dozen such children.

In planning their lives as radical Christians, the Gauchats followed the light of the gospel as it was opened to them from the start. They did not plan to open a house of hospitality for children with disabilities. Yet, unknown to them, their future work had been built into the way they organized their lives. Their concept of family required them to make space for the stranger at the gate. That is the kind of community Jesus talks about. He does not care whether it is built around a biological family or an intentional community or an informal circle of friends.

Lesbians and gay men are familiar with this. Those of us who have lost birth families can partake of a long tradition of making new families. The circles of friends we come to know in Armistead Maupin's *Tales of the City* series are lovely and hilarious examples. The demands of caring for people with AIDS have strengthened this older tradition. The practice of some lesbian couples who enlist the regular support of gay male couples in raising their male children—a kind of four-parent family—could also serve as a model for those social critics casting about for antidotes to the single-working-mother family pattern.

Jesus, though he pointed the way, never had this kind of family. The community he tried to build during his ministry disintegrated at his arrest, and Jesus himself suffered the isolation he tried to counteract. This is what we relive in the liturgy of the Triduum, the three holy days that are the climax of Lent and Holy Week. Two events of Holy Week hint at the cause of his community's disintegration. The triumphal entry into Jerusalem reminds us, first, how much we want to have someone else do it all for us. We want a king who will throw out the Romans. But then, Judas's attempt to manipulate events so that they would go according to his plan is the other side of that coin, the second cause. It reminds us how much we want to take everything on ourselves.

When we leave everything to someone else, or when we try to do it all by ourselves, we fail. Instead of working together, instead of knowing ourselves as the image of God and living our lives after the pattern of the everflowing love of the Trinity, we leave Jesus alone in Gethsemane. We utter Peter's denial. We join the flight of the male disciples. In their flight, indeed, is another lesson: men are expected to go it alone, and it is the men who flee. The women remain. So does John, who has stood at the foot of the cross throughout Christian history, a model of the love of two men for one another.

Jesus, too, must have felt his love rejected, sharing the pain that I know all too well. But we gay men and lesbians know something else, too, which we risk rejection to share. We know that love has power. The lesbian liberation theologian Carter Heyward puts it this way: "*The power in relation is God*" [her italics]. She goes on to call this understanding "so foreign to traditional Christian thought that [it] necessitates . . . new symbols, or images, by which we might express the value of shared power."[13]

"The power of love" is a phrase that Christians use so easily it has turned to candy. It is sweet, it drips like honey from our lips, leaving no nourishment behind. Lesbians and gay men still feel the truth of that power. If love had no power, it would not be forbidden, as for us it is forbidden. The impulse to love is so powerful it must be dammed. We know something else too, having so much practice at blocking off our loving impulses: love dammed up is all the stronger when set free.

This truth is shown us in the garden of Gethsemane. Jesus was left alone by his sleeping disciples, and in his abandonment he prayed to be relieved of his burden. The force of his love had been blocked by indifference and sleep, even among the ones he had tried to build into a community of love. Did he think of Lazarus then, the one he loved so much that he could not do without him and so brought him back from the dead? If Jesus' love could bring Lazarus back, how can it be confined by a tomb?

CHAPTER 4

What God Has
Made Clean

I am an insurgent. I rebel against the existing situation,
because I hold it to be a condition of injustice. I fight for
freedom from persecution and insults. I call for recognition of Urning love. I call for it from public opinion and
from the State. As inborn Dioning love is recognized as
just by public opinion and the State, so too I demand from
both the recognition that inborn Urning sexual love is just.
—Numa Numantius (Karl Heinrich Ulrichs), *Vindicta*[1]

In chapter 3 I discussed the importance of moving
beyond individual salvation to an understanding that we have life
and humanity only in relation to one another. This requires
breaking out of rote interactions with our sisters and brothers and
relating to one another as individuals, something lesbians and gay
men learn as a matter of survival.

We saw, though, that this might not be enough. Jesus tried to
build a community of such people, but they abandoned him in the
end. Something was missing; something, it turns out, only living
together as church would bring into being. The resurrection
created a sense of belonging to a group, a sense of holy community.
The Jesus movement grew into a community as it had to define
itself as different from the society around it, in particular, as its
members tried to understand why society saw their new community as a threat. They had to move through friendship to solidarity.
This process is recognizable from recent history as the development
of class consciousness.

Early Christians also saw the growth of the community in the
light of history. The liturgy, which so often restores the balance
thrown off by the weightiness of verbal theology, has always linked
the resurrection with the exodus, seeing each as a moment of
liberation from slavery, a time when God's mighty hand reached

into history to transform it. At the Roman Catholic Easter vigil, the deacon sings over the new-lit Paschal candle the history of salvation:

> This is our passover feast, when Christ, the true Lamb, is slain, whose blood consecrates the homes of all believers. This is the night when . . . you freed the people of Israel from their slavery and led them dry-shod through the sea. . . . This is the night when Jesus Christ broke the chains of death and rose triumphant from the grave.[2]

Just as I have considered the exodus experience through the eyes of a gay man, now it is time to view the making of the church from the same perspective. As the wandering in the desert made a rabble into a people for God, and as the life of the resurrection church made another rabble into another people for God, the struggle to create a liberation force out of the tag ends of sexual dissidence is forming a class of lesbian and gay male people.

That this process is incomplete is made clear by our lack of a term to describe what we are becoming. We once spoke of the homophile and then of the gay community. We came to understand that women were invisible in such catch-all terms and began to speak of a lesbian/gay community. But we are really a number of communities, not yet a class. A more recent term, associated in many minds with a loose organization but really meaning much more, is a Queer Nation; but many of us have difficulty with the idea of nationalism, and it is far from clear who or what is comprehended by the word "queer."

Comparing lesbians and gay men in our present society with the making of a people for God, whether at Sinai or in the cities of the Roman Empire, no doubt seems to many people almost obscene. But making a people out of a bunch of slaves and social misfits undoubtedly seemed as ungodly to the Pharisees as the idea of building a lesbian and gay people to be a people of God does today. One of the main complaints of Roman officials about the new Christian sect, in fact, was that it attracted the offscourings of society.

Over time, that mob was turned into a people. Israel became a nation, and Israel was clean. The mark of distinction between Israel and everyone else found most often in scripture is the distinction between clean and unclean. That is what the book of Leviticus is about: its catalogue of rules, including the fierce condemnation of sex between males, is a way to keep "us" separate from "them."

Eating and Touching,
Otherness and Identity

Drawing parallels between the lesbian and gay community and Israel seems wrong because lesbians and gay men are still unclean by the rules of our society. We are outcasts, people whose presence (if known) is polluting, discussion of whom in a school curriculum will somehow corrupt the children exposed to it. During the last decade, the spread of AIDS has only made this sentiment more vicious.

It is not only other people who feel this way about us. We do too, at least occasionally. This is one reason why coming out and naming our oppression are both crucial steps, and why many gay men never take them. It is why we need a gay liberation theology. We will never be able to decide what an authentically Christian gay life is as long as we believe we are unworthy to construct it ourselves.

All oppressed people share the experience of accepting some of the oppressor's terms of reference. That is how we are coopted into going along with our oppression. So, for many gay men, our sense of uncleanness, of deserving to be outcasts, is very strong. It keeps us from hearing the good news of liberation.

One of the classic ways in which people are kept out, whatever the basis for divisions in any given society, is to make them untouchable, literally or figuratively. In the case of class divisions, people are made untouchable by making sure they are on the other side of the tracks. "Good" people do not come into contact with them, because they are separated by geography. That's what suburbs do, too.

AIDS has increased our untouchability. We have all seen photographs of police wearing gloves at gay rights demonstrations. I recall one delightful reversal of this during the Supreme Court civil disobedience in 1987. At earlier demonstrations for AIDS funding, the Washington, D.C., police had worn bright yellow gloves. (For the Supreme Court action, they switched to more discreet clear plastic ones.) One affinity group of gay men from Boston, the United Fruit Company (which started out doing Central America solidarity work), offered themselves for arrest wearing identical pillbox hats, with little veils in front, and yellow rubber gloves. As they crossed the street from the Capitol lawn to the Supreme Court, they shook their fingers at the police and chanted, "Your gloves don't match your shoes! Your gloves don't match your shoes!"

Their joke had a sharp point. Despite all the education for a decade on modes of HIV transmission, lesbians and gay men are often literally untouchables. I have experienced this treatment myself, even at mass. The custom among Catholic Worker types is to move around the living room (or wherever the Eucharist is being celebrated) for the Kiss of Peace, hugging one another. Too many times, I have been greeted instead by a handshake.

In 1991 and 1992, there were widespread protests against a restaurant chain for firing lesbians and gay men as a matter of policy. Counterdemonstrators and patrons told the press that it was right to exclude lesbians and gay men from working in restaurants because they would contaminate the food they touched with the AIDS virus. There have even been reports—fewer lately—of debates in churches over whether to allow people with HIV to take Communion from the common cup.

These last two examples repeat a classic pattern of separation: laws specifying with whom you can eat. In the caste system in India, it is the test of one's standing in the hierarchy. Brahmans may accept food only from Brahmans; Kshatriyas, the next lower caste, only from Brahmans or Kshatriyas; and so on. I still remember laws in this country that prevented people of color from eating with white people and drinking from the same water fountain.

Similar prohibitions have historically been used (thinly veiled) in dealing with people caught having "unnatural" sex. Literary historian Louis Crompton documents the historical rigidity of British society, abroad as well as in the islands of the United Kingdom, in excluding from the table those accused of buggery— those not hanged, that is. One "gentleman," for instance, had to account for having toured the house of the notorious sodomite William Beckford in 1806, before he could be invited to dinner again.[3]

Separation can become a tool of resistance. As the system of marks separating Israel from the nations was constructed, the prohibition against eating together became important in defining the community. At the time of Jesus, good Jews did not eat with Gentiles; remember the Samaritan woman's surprise at Jesus' asking her for water. This was one of the few ways in which Jews could resist assimilation into the Roman Empire: They lived in an occupied country, after all. A contemporary parallel is the lesbian separatist belief that unless and until lesbians have developed an autonomous culture and society, they will continue to be subordinated not only to men in general but also to gay men within the movement for sexual liberation. In such cases, separation has dual ends: consciousness building and creating a material base from which to struggle for liberation.

Identity and Class Consciousness

The question "What kind of group are we?" has been lying just beneath the surface of the lesbian and gay male movements ever since the beginnings of organizing activities in the late 1940s. Only occasionally has it come to the surface, where it could be debated. One period when it did was during the rapid expansion of organizing that accompanied Stonewall. I say "accompanied" rather than the more usual "followed" because new approaches and new organizations had begun at least one to three years earlier, depending on how one conceives of the political developments of the sixties. In fact, a strong argument could be made that the new energy made Stonewall, not the other way around.[4] In any case, I believe that Stonewall, like the passage through the Red Sea, is best thought of as a symbolic moment in the midst of a tide of political activity, when at last the possibility of genuine passage to liberation suddenly was seen to be open by large groups of lesbians and gay men.

The politics of the time were such that tensions developed between activists who looked to more traditional kinds of organizing and those who looked to a change in consciousness.[5] This had two effects. One was the beginnings of lesbian separatism, which has enjoyed a rich history. The other, more limited in scope and thus easier to summarize, was the split between the Gay Liberation Front (GLF) and the Gay Activists Alliance (GAA).

Drastically oversimplified, this split was a conflict over whether gay people (as the term then was—the invisibility of women in the phrase reflects the silence that convinced many lesbians of the need for separatism) should work primarily within other New Left groups or should concentrate exclusively on lesbian and gay issues. In a 1972 interview, Arthur Evans, one of the leaders of the secession that created GAA, clarified the difference. The gay liberation movement was still in its first stages, he pointed out. Organizing around issues of immediate interest to large numbers of lesbians and gay men, such as job discrimination and harassment by police, had to take priority. Not only were the issues important in themselves; organizing around them would create a sense of common purpose and political power among previously isolated individuals. "The exact fights won't matter. . . . We have to have our identity. We don't have our identity yet. The gay community isn't a community yet."[6]

Implicit in this analysis is a critique of the GLF position, which on its face was more "revolutionary." GLF was very loosely organized and stood for a visible gay presence in the movements against the war in Southeast Asia and racism at home. Relations with the Black Panther Party were a major focus. GLF took part in such events as the Revolutionary People's Constitutional Convention in Philadelphia in September 1970. Marxist language was prominent in GLF writing.

The two positions should not be too sharply differentiated; they reflected more a difference in tactics than in long-range goals. A second look at them reveals that Evans's position was, in fact, more classically Marxist. Although the term was little used either in the GLF–GAA debates or in the internal literary discussion carried on in the Socialist Workers Party (SWP) shortly thereafter, what Evans identified was the need to develop a class consciousness among lesbians and gay men.

This task has yet to be faced head-on. As I mentioned, considerable ink has been spilled in recent years over whether there is or is not a "gay community" or a "lesbian and gay community" and, if there is, who is included. Part of the difficulty is that the concept of "community" is not precise enough to be of much use as a tool of political analysis. Moreover, it brings with it unexplored additional baggage in its connotations of emotional comfort and cultural unity. We expect to feel at home in a community, and prejudice, cultural conflict, and political opposition disillusion us when we encounter them there. Among members of a "class," however, such things can be seen as part of the struggle.

Our unwillingness to think about ourselves as a developing class is, I suspect, the result of the overwhelmingly middle-class character of recent U.S. lesbian and gay male politics and the conservatism of U.S. politics generally. The myth that the United States has no classes or that all of us are middle-class has stunted our ability to reason about society.[7] Avoidance is made easier when we have no language to use. Marxists speak of "the working class." The term describes what the people who belong to it do. Neither "gay," "lesbian," nor the newer word "queer" describes a social function.

Another linguistic obstacle is the variety of uses to which we put the word "class" in our political thought. There are three ways in which we commonly use the word: as a category of Marxist analysis, as a sociological term, and as a concept in civil rights law. The first two are very imprecisely distinguished from each other, and the myth that ours is a classless society abets the imprecision. The last use of the term is fairly precise but rarely understood: I refer to the idea of a "protected class," whose members are presumed, by the fact of belonging to it, to suffer routinely the denial of rights that they possess in theory. This is what antidiscrimination laws are about. The current debate over such legislation covering lesbians and gay men, like the 1992 amendment to the Colorado constitution that forbids protection of our civil rights, has gone far astray. This is partly the result of a deliberate strategy by the opponents of all civil rights legislation to cast such laws as "special rights"; and it is partly a failure of proponents of lesbian and gay civil rights legislation to articulate clearly what a "protected class" is. The more fundamental problem of who belongs to such a class and thus who is protected by lesbian and gay civil rights legislation has been ignored because our jurisprudence typically leaves such matters to the development of case law. A more focused discussion of the concept of a functionally named class, whatever we end up calling it, might help forestall future problems. (It might also put the essentialist–constructionist debate on a more concrete foundation.)

An obvious place to look for models for such a class is "the making of the working class," to borrow the title of British historian E. P. Thompson's study of that process in England. His preface contains a number of valuable observations, primary among which is the understanding that "the working class did not rise like the sun at an appointed time. It was present at its own making."[8] This is a historical process, the result of concrete and specific interactions between groups of real people. If we substitute our recent history for that of the English working class, we end up with a rather helpful proposition: lesbians and gay men, between 1945 and 1995, recognized their interests as a group, in solidarity with each other and in opposition to the guardians of capitalist morality.[9] Thompson goes on to point out that this guardian class, in church and state, was itself divided and, indeed, only overcame—or agreed to ignore—its divisions because it needed unity against the rising working class. In our current circumstances, the same is true of the divisions between fundamentalist and Catholic Christians, between separatist Christians and political parties, or between Republicans who believe in individual liberty and those wishing to use the party to create a Christian commonwealth, all of which must be papered over in order to resist lesbian and gay male demands for sexual freedom.[10]

Central to Thompson's thesis is his conviction, which, as a believer in a God of history, I can only share, that "the notion of class entails the notion of historical relationship. Like any other relationship, it is a fluency which evades analysis if we attempt to stop it dead at any given moment and anatomise its structure. The finest-meshed sociological net cannot give us a pure specimen of class, any more than it can give us one of deference or of love. The relationship must always be embodied in real people and in a real context."[11] This is opposed to the "ever-present temptation to suppose that class is a thing."[12] Most Marxist "vanguard" parties, debating about "homosexuality," have yielded to this temptation, as can be seen in the SWP discussion mentioned above. For Thompson—and, he maintains, for Marx as well—"class is defined by men as they live their own history, and, in the end, this is its only definition."[13]

We stand midstream in this historical process. That complicates our view of where the process is going, even of how far along we are. I suggest that we are poised at the moment where we have achieved a consciousness of being an oppressed class but have yet to be able to discern how to put this consciousness to political use. Our political lack of clarity, in fact, is probably a sign that our class consciousness is not fully formed, if such a thing ever is. We have not yet come to consensus on what our liberation should look like. If we do not, we risk seeing our sense of class pulled apart by the gravitational forces exerted by the other identities—race, gender, economic class—that divide us.

Economic Oppression and Exploitation

To build such a consensus, however, we need to identify more clearly the basis of our oppression. So far we have tended to do this by looking too much at the superstructure and too little at the base, that is, by identifying homophobia as a cultural relic—the inheritance of Christian antigay sentiment, perhaps. It is more useful to examine what function our oppression serves in a capitalist system. After all, as we have already learned, the fairly recent category of "homosexual" was adopted as part of constructing capitalist social relations. We must get past thinking of ourselves as victims of irrational prejudice and start thinking of ourselves as exploited.

Fundamental to an understanding of exploitation is the concept of the division of labor. The function lesbians and gay men serve in the division of labor is not clear, and the question is really the matter for another whole book. Some attempts have been made to answer it, notably by David Thorstad and John Lauritsen in the SWP debate. I look at Lauritsen's analysis presently.

First, it may help us to look at a parallel case: the function people with disabilities serve in the division of labor. We should expect our cases to be parallel, since "homosexuality" took shape as a medical concept. We could understand it, in fact, as a branch of the trunk from which other disability groups also grow.[14]

People with disabilities with whom I have done political work express to me, with growing frequency, the conviction that their function in capitalist society is to warn workers against complaining about working conditions, wages, safety, and the like. The unspoken message is "Be thankful you can work. Look at those pitiful folks who can't." Hidden beneath the warning, of course, is the threat "And we can make sure you can't work either"; hence the popularity of what many radical people with disabilities call "pity parties": spectacles such as the Labor Day telethon to raise money for "Jerry's kids" with muscular dystrophy. The fact that many of these "kids" are adults with jobs and independent lives is carefully hidden, just as are many facts about lesbian and gay male lives.

This is one aspect of what is called "the reserve army of labor." Some amount of unemployment is useful to owners and managers to keep wages low and workers in line. In the 1972 SWP debate, John Lauritsen connected this phenomenon to the exploitation of lesbians and gay men. Referring to "the extremes business and government will go to in hunting out gays"—less so twenty years later, perhaps, although the debate over discharging lesbian and gay male members of the armed forces has reminded us that it still takes place—Lauritsen writes:

> When gays are found out and fired, they not only join the reserve army of labor, they join it permanently. Either that, or they find employment only in a lower paid or in a totally different field than the one they left. Women, etc., are hired in periods of prosperity and let go during depressions. That's how the reserve army of labor works. But gays, once found out and fired, are finished. . . . The threat of being discovered and becoming a marginal person is always there."[15]

It is important to realize that this is not just about controlling lesbians and gay men. Homophobic attacks, Lauritsen reminds us, keep everyone in line, since "a white male worker is not going to turn in a Black or a woman. He has no guarantee, however, that he will never be labeled as 'queer.' . . . Straight equals conforming. Gay equals stepping out of line. To be straight, workers support the war in Vietnam. They wear American flags as badges of their heterosexuality. Because of fear and prejudice revolving around gays, they support capitalism, in which they have no objective stake whatever."[16]

One reason we have been slow to examine the material basis of our exploitation goes back to the debate I discussed in the Introduction about whether lesbian and gay male identities are essences or social constructs. This shows up at the tactical level when we consider such matters as whether to speak of sexual "preference" or "orientation" or in debating whether gayness is an unchangeable condition or a freely chosen "lifestyle."

Lesbians and gay men have put a lot of eggs in the born-that-way basket, based on a faulty understanding of the concept of a protected class. We have based our politics on an analogy between sexual orientation and gender or race. This has led us to believe that the only way to secure our rights is to argue that gayness is innate. To do this, we have to deny the experiences of many of us, who may, for example, have lived in heterosexual marriages for some time before they came out.

Innateness is not a necessary condition of becoming a protected class. Religion, for example, is a classic protected choice in our civil rights tradition; so is political belief. Both categories, in fact, have a longer history of protection than either gender or race. The failure to ratify the Equal Rights Amendment should teach us that Americans are not altogether sure that just because a characteristic is "inborn" it is necessarily neutral. In the long run, protection as a class can be won only by political struggle. There are no shortcuts.

In Defense of Exploitation: Bourgeois Religion

What might theology have to teach us on these issues? Jesus' followers found themselves confronting similar ones in trying to understand the resurrection. It may help us to see the situations as parallel to contrast theologian J. B. Metz's bourgeois religion with some experiences of the early church as related in Acts. Then we will be able to consider the resurrection itself in chapter 5.

Metz's description of bourgeois religion has a particular aptness for lesbians and gay men. Accepting the norms of society in place of the promises of the gospel has deprived religion of any "messianic future": "The bourgeois virtues of stability, competitive struggle, and achievement obscure and overlay the . . . messianic virtues of conversion, selfless and unconditional love for the 'least of the brethren,' and active compassion—virtues which cannot be practiced within relationships of exchange or barter; virtues for which one gets literally nothing in return."[17] Not all lesbian and gay male love, of course, is messianic, but as we saw in chapter 3, the fact that we must persist in the face of society's hatred suggests that our love threatens the comfort of the bourgeoisie.

We can recognize the effects of bourgeois religion most clearly in the bourgeois family, but Metz also sees it in our fondness for cheap reconciliation.

> Does not the concept of universal Christian love lose all its dynamism and tension under the spell of bourgeois religion? Is this perhaps the reason it scarcely needs to prove itself any more as love of the enemy, since in the feeble and nonpartisan way in which it bridges over all agonizing contradictions, it manages not to have any real enemies at all? . . . Underneath the priorities of the gospel, the priorities of bourgeois life are being practiced."[18]

First among these priorities is respectability, the code that defines middle-class status. We have tried to make a church of the already pure. Rather than preach the possibilities of a radical faith, Metz tells us, the church has turned to rigorism—rigidity in both doctrine and discipline—to maintain its failing influence. This is not peculiar to Catholicism; it underlies the controversy over the ordination of openly lesbian and gay male candidates in a number of liberal Protestant denominations. The disciplines being adopted— and increasingly defied—imply a two-tiered membership that is at odds with the central Protestant insight of the priesthood of all believers. The pews are open to all; the ministry is open only to the pure, the clean, the respectable.

This results in the narrowing Metz denounces: a model of church as bourgeois family writ large. And we know, from theologian Dorothee Soelle, where this leads: "The loving fathers who ran the gas chambers of Auschwitz symbolize the dreadful end of this bourgeois experiment."[19] As long as they loved their wives and children according to the dictates of bourgeois religion, they could do as they liked to everyone else—and still receive the sacraments. The church opens its door to this when it allows some people to be classed as unclean, as less than human, as deserving of the grisly deaths prescribed by Leviticus and, as we shall see, rejected by the early church.

Bourgeois religion made Adolf Hitler's Final Solution possible. It consoled the loving fathers by assuring them that the people they were "solving" at Treblinka and Dachau and Flossenbürg were not people at all; they were outside the narrow limits the state had redrawn in an amazingly short period of time. The institutions of the state, including state churches, acquiesced in the redefinition of clean humanity. The bourgeoisie were still safe inside this definition. So, if only by its silence, bourgeois religion permitted the state to call its actions justice.

This should not surprise us. Bourgeois religion, as Soelle and Metz describe it, has also adopted bourgeois concepts of justice, which are not so different from bourgeois ideas of love. Rigorism, after all, emphasizes primacy of justice over mercy. Bourgeois justice is based on a person's deserts—put more baldly, on a person's productive or reproductive capacity.

Rejecting Respectability

Against bourgeois ideas of love and justice, Soelle offers us the person of Mary. Why is the mother of God so visible in popular piety, so revered by outcasts of all kinds? "Mary rejects 'performance' as a measure of human value. . . . Her unconditional acceptance is that of a mother who cannot exchange her child in the store if she finds it doesn't suit her. If we strip charity of sentimentality, the 'amoral' quality that it originally had becomes visible again. And it is for this kind of amorality that the Mary of legends and folks tales has a mischievous penchant."[20]

Matthew 20:1–16

An excellent scriptural example of Soelle's "amoral quality of charity" is a parable of the laborers in the vineyard (Matt. 20:1–16). God's commonwealth is "like a landowner who went out early in the morning to hire laborers for his vineyard." Jesus tells how the owner kept hiring more workers throughout the day; when he ordered that they be paid the same regardless of hours worked, there was understandable grumbling. His reply sounds odd to twentieth-century ears:

> Friend, I am doing you no wrong; did you not agree with me for the usual daily wage? Take what belongs to you and go; I choose to give to this last the same as I give to you. Am I not allowed to do what I choose with what belongs to me? Or are you envious because I am generous?

"So," Jesus sums up, "the last will be first and the first will be last."

When I read this parable, my first instinct is to imagine it being used to justify union busting. The landowner's statement that he is free to do whatever he wants with his money grates on me: it is so like the smug capitalist demand that no restrictions be placed on free trade. But the moral that Jesus draws from the parable stands the facts on their head. He forces us to look at the story again, and it now seems to offer little comfort to capitalist production. These workers are not just items in a balance sheet. They are paid according to their innate worth as human beings, not according to how much they produced. The last workers may not have produced anything at all; but they are not valued in terms of productivity. This owner would be laughed out of Congress: what he is proposing is that everybody deserves a minimum guaranteed income and that jobs must be created with this in mind—this and the dignity of the worker. He goes far beyond the demands for full employment that today seem so utopian as to have vanished from serious political discussion. (Remember the reserve army of labor?) Justice here is not based on anybody's deserts. Seen from the point of view of bourgeois society, this justice has the amoral quality that Soelle ascribes to Mary.

Unlike Mary, the church has accepted society's categories and, with them, the task of controlling the definition of whom God loves. In short, the church conforms itself to this world not in working for the liberation of lesbians and gay men but in consenting to become an accomplice of the state in repressing it.[21] In this situation, the church, if it hopes to recover its prophetic role, needs lesbians and gay men, not the other way around. In this society, we are the authorities on the limits to God's love. The very idea is shocking: limits to God's love! But lesbians and gay men have been placed outside those supposed limits—we know where they are. The church will not certify that we have been made "clean" unless we can prove that we have met certain social requirements that did not exist until bourgeois society invented them in order to discover us.

But what was Jesus' practice? How did Jesus deal with the unclean, the impure, the outcasts, the bad people of society? It is not easy for us to recover this, because we read the gospel with the eyes of the church. So we no longer recognize the "good" people of society when we read about the Pharisees, for instance; we think of them as hypocrites, "bad" people. But in their own time and place, the Pharisees were the best people. They stood for faithfulness to God, rather than conformity to the Greek world that was increasingly infiltrating Palestine.

It was precisely these respectable, even holy, people whom Jesus was hardest on. It was precisely the ones they despised with whom he spent his time: people whose lives were not ordered toward discerning God's ends but instead were, to use the Roman Catholic Church's terminology, "intrinsically disordered."

Luke 7:36–50

One story illustrating this appears in all four Gospels in different versions. The version I look at here is found in Luke 7:36–50, because this is the version where Jesus' feet are anointed by a woman we have come to know as a "harlot." In John, it is Mary of Bethany who anoints Jesus; by a series of shaky identifications, this is the origin of our picture of Mary Magdalene as a reformed prostitute.

Closer reading of Luke reveals that the woman is described not as a harlot but as a sinner. The nature of her sins is not given. We have read into the story our assumption, probably because she is a woman, that they are sexual. The other versions, focusing on the costliness of the ointment, do not even raise the issue of the woman's character; but Matthew and Mark add the interesting information that the host is untouchable: they name him "Simon the leper" (Matt. 26:6; Mark 14:3). Luke chooses to emphasize the contrast between the respectable host and the loving action of the outcast: "When the Pharisee who had invited him saw it, he said to himself, 'If this man were a prophet, he would have known who and what kind of woman this is who is touching him—that she is a sinner' " (Luke 7:39). Jesus' response in pointed:

> Do you see this woman? I entered your house; you gave me no water for my feet, but she has bathed my feet with her tears and dried them with her hair. You gave me no kiss, but from the time I came in she has

not stopped kissing my feet. You did not anoint my head with oil, but she has anointed my feet with ointment. Therefore I tell you, her sins, which were many, have been forgiven; hence she has shown great love. But the one to whom little is forgiven, loves little. (Luke 7:44–47)

There are a couple of ways to read this story. If Simon was a leper, he would be expected to omit the customary courtesies, to avoid contaminating his guest. With this understanding, Jesus would be gently urging Simon to respect himself, not to seek others' approval. Luke, identifying Simon only as a Pharisee, is more critical; here the emphasis is on social position, even, one might say, social class. Simon's omission of those duties of hospitality that Jesus names shows what the Pharisee really thinks of this upstart claiming to be a teacher and prophet. A good Pharisee would not risk his respectability by touching someone who might not keep kosher. (The turn-of-the-century American master critic and prose writer William Dean Howells once called one of his characters' respectability "the wish to be honored for what he seemed.")[22] His respectability might be great; but his love is small, and his sins are not forgiven.

Luke 19:1–10

Another visit Jesus makes is to a tax collector named Zacchaeus. In this case, the "parade" is Jesus entering Jericho.

[Zacchaeus] was trying to see who Jesus was, but on account of the crowd he could not, because he was short in stature. So he ran ahead and climbed a sycamore tree to see him, because he was going to pass that way. When Jesus came to the place, he looked up and said to him, "Zacchaeus, hurry and come down; for I must stay at your house today." So he hurried down and was happy to welcome him. All who saw it began to grumble and said, "He has gone to be the guest of one who is a sinner." Zacchaeus stood there and said to the Lord, "Look, half of my possessions, Lord, I will give to the poor; and if I have defrauded anyone of anything, I will pay back four times as much." Then Jesus said to him, "Today salvation has come to this house, because he too is a son of Abraham. For the Son of Man came to seek out and save the lost."

This visit, as well as the visit to Simon, is to an outcast. In both cases, Jesus' preaching tours are not to the respectable folks of the locality but to those excluded by the respectable people, a leper and a tax gatherer (Simon may be a Pharisee, but that does not seem to count for much with Jesus). Notice, too, that Jesus makes no exhortation to reform. He never says to the woman, any more than he did to the woman at the well of Samaria, "Go and sin no more"; nor does he say it to Zacchaeus, who makes his gesture of conversion without prompting.

It is a fine gesture. Remember how tax collection worked under the Roman Empire. A person like Zacchaeus would bid for the right to collect taxes. Once possessed of it, he would then extort more tax than his bid so as to make a profit, which he kept. Many *publicani*, as they were called, made fortunes this way. It was a kind of legal racketeering; hence the murmur "He has gone to the house of a sinner."

But Zacchaeus does not resign his post. He simply agrees not to make a profit from it. Giving away half of what he has to the poor suggests that he has made a lot of money of which he now wants to disembarrass himself. Furthermore, he is going to make fourfold restitution. This is not simply bourgeois justice; he is paying back more than he owes by strict calculation, even if we include interest and penalties. Here, too, as in the case of the woman who anoints Jesus, we see an outpouring of love, and in this case, it is of a more practical kind. Zacchaeus shows his love for Jesus by an act of generosity toward his neighbors.

Redeeming Our Class

By such acts of love are the outcasts redeemed. This is radical love, not the rigorism that the churches use toward lesbians and gay men. For all the sugarcoating and beating around the bush, the churches' message comes through to us loud and clear: "God loves you but does not love your sexual practices. Therefore, if you stop them— what's more, if you stop associating with other lesbians and gay men, so you won't be tempted to start again—and instead make yourselves as much like us as possible, only celibate, of course, then we will know you have become clean enough to associate with us. But whatever you do, don't try to work this out by yourselves, because your impulses are 'intrinsically disordered' and you can no longer think straight."

But if the category of "the homosexual" is socially constructed— which means politically constructed—like other classes, then it is a case of dealing not with individual sinners but with social groups. There seems to be a feeling abroad, among lesbians and gay men as well as others, that if "homosexuality" is a social construct, it is somehow not a real category; that women who desired women and men who desired men did not exist before the nineteenth century. This, of course, is not what it means. There may not have been an "English working class" before the period that E. P. Thompson chronicles, but there certainly were stockingers and weavers and cutlery makers. What changed was their position in society and their understanding of that position.

Similarly, there may have been no "homosexuals" in the time of Jesus. I believe there were none, and therefore I do not expect scripture to tell us anything about them directly. It may tell us about the devotees of Aphrodite at Corinth or Adonis at Rome; but none of them is alive anymore. Scripture can tell us about tax collectors and Samaritans, both of them outcast groups in the society in which Jesus lived, as the Gospels show us repeatedly. Jesus did not tell the Samaritan woman to stop being Samaritan: he led her to a truth that went beyond the categories "Samaritan" or "Jew." He did not tell Zacchaeus to stop being a tax collector: he praised him for trying to work out, on the basis of his own life situation, a way to live more justly within the category.

The category of "publican" would not have gone away no matter how many individuals Jesus converted. If Zacchaeus had quit his job, another, greedier man would have taken his place, because the Romans needed such a class of people to raise money to run the empire. The only way to abolish the category or some equally unjust (because equally imperialist) structure a Roman reform party might have put in its place was to abolish the empire.

Just so, there is no way to abolish the category of "the homosexual" under bourgeois society. It serves a function in the maintenance of that order. Furthermore, it serves that function as the negative to the positive category of "the heterosexual." You cannot abolish one without abolishing the other, because each exists to define the other. All you can do is make the categories irrelevant. This was precisely the revolutionary aim proclaimed by early gay liberation groups.

This is the contradiction inherent in the "family-values" movement: it wants to abolish the category "homosexual" in order to save the bourgeois (heterosexual) family; but it cannot succeed without abolishing heterosexuality too. The best it can hope to do is abolish individual homosexuals. That way lies the Final Solution. This fits the observations made by Karl Marx and Friedrich Engels: "Each new class which puts itself in the place of the one ruling before it, is compelled, merely in order to carry through its aim, to

represent its interest as the common interest of all the members of
society, put in an ideal form; it will give its ideas the form of
universality, and represent them as the only rational, universally
valid ones."[23]

This is precisely what has happened with the family as it is
portrayed by the family-values activists. It is God-given (thus
universally valid), and until "militant homosexuals"—not so long
ago, it was godless Communists—attempted to destroy it, everybody lived in one. It has no history because it has always existed in
the same form, only now it is decked out with more modern
appliances. The few who are too poor to live in one must be helped
to do so by becoming better bourgeois, for it is in the common
interest of the whole society for them to buy more modern
appliances too. Joseph and Mary and Jesus have been dragged into
the picture: the Holy Family might just as well have lived in a
suburb of Kansas City as in Nazareth. The history of the bourgeois
family and its relation to the workings of the Industrial Revolution
and of modern consumer capitalism has vanished. "Natural" sex,
too, becomes the kind that is most compatible with this "natural"
social institution. Calling both natural lets us pretend they have
nothing to do with rule by a certain class.

The Fallacy of Pure Identity

But if Metz is right that when Christian love is lived only in the
family, it soon becomes impossible to live it even there, then
perhaps the task of Christians is to work out, like Zacchaeus, some
new way of inhabiting the categories "homosexual" and "heterosexual" on the basis of our own life situations. Because these
categories depend on each other for existence, this work can only
be done by all of us, in solidarity. It is a revolutionary work: it will
lead, one day, to the end of heterosexuality as well as of homosexuality. And it will be finished only when neither category serves the
function of class rule—perhaps, as early gay liberationists declared,
only when there is no more class rule.

Ruth

This work done in solidarity is likely to turn our own categories
on their heads and leave us wondering where we fit. The good
news has always had this quality, which is why parables played such

an important part in Jesus' preaching. We may take comfort in our confusion from the story of Ruth and Naomi, which mixes everything up. This couple is claimed both by straights—at weddings, for instance—and by lesbians, since Ruth's love for her mother-in-law is clearly the central attachment of the tale, not her love for her husband.

In its original context, the book of Ruth is a story about welcoming outsiders. Naomi is the widow of an expatriate, a certain Elimelech, who left Bethlehem to live in Moab and promptly died, leaving Naomi a single mother. Her two sons in the fullness of time married local women and then, some ten years later, died also, childless, leaving three women on their own.

We can imagine that by that time the family was as much Moabite as Judahite; but there is only one course open for Naomi, who is obviously a strong and resourceful woman: to go back to her people in Judah, a nearly forgotten poor relation, hardly more than a beggar. Small wonder, then, that Naomi urges her daughters-in-law not to join her. Orpah sees reason; Ruth chooses love.

"Do not press me to leave you or to turn back from following you! Where you go, I will go; where you lodge, I will lodge; your people shall be my people, and your God my God. Where you die, I will die—there will I be buried" (Ruth 1:16–17). This willingness to abandon everything and risk an uncertain future for love is what makes the story so powerful and so beloved. Indeed, lesbians' and gay men's special fondness for this story, based on its picture of the love of two women, can hardly surpass that of our straight sisters and brothers. But the book's function in the canon of scripture is slightly different from any of our contemporary readings; it is an anonymous writer's reminder, at a time when the Jewish people were busy setting themselves off from others by means of the minutiae of ritual purity, that the great king David was the great-grandson of a foreign woman. Ruth was a Moabite. Who knows what kind of food she ate before she accompanied Naomi home? For that matter, how could anyone be sure that Naomi herself, long in foreign parts, had not stooped to eating filthy meat?

Yet the survival strategy these two devised would change history. Ruth attracted the notice of the wealthy kinsman of Naomi's dead husband, who was fulfilling his obligation to help her feed herself by gleaning in his fields. And what attracted his notice? Ruth, we may guess, was not young by the standards of the time: she had been married ten years, though we can suppose she married young. She was childless, we know, but that does not mean she never faced the rigors of childbirth. The romance of love at first sight is in the tale, to be sure, but the reason Boaz speaks to her is not what we would expect: "All that you have done for your mother-in-law since the death of your husband has been fully told me, and how you left your father and mother and your native land and came to a people that you did not know before" (Ruth 2:11). He begs God for a blessing on her. He himself is to be the means of its fulfillment; for he marries her and begets a son for these motherless widows: not just any son, either, but the father of Jesse, who would be the father of David, the great king.

And who is this Boaz? Matthew tells us in his genealogy of Jesus, where Ruth is one of the few women named. Boaz's mother is also named there: Rahab, whom we met at the fall of Jericho. Jesus is of the house of David, descended through him from outsiders.

In *The Future Is Mestizo*, the Texan priest Virgil Elizondo puts Jesus' marginality at the center of his ministry. To begin with, Elizondo notes, all Galileans had a mixed, or *mestizo*, heritage: "The Jews in Galilee were too Jewish to be accepted by the Gentile population and too contaminated with pagan ways to be accepted by the pure-minded Jews of Jerusalem."[24] This reality would have struck Jesus' hearers and, later, those who heard his Galilean companions preaching every time they spoke: after all, Peter's accent betrayed his lie when he denied Jesus.

Elizondo makes this generalized ethnic impurity personal to Jesus:

> Was not the father of Jesus a Roman soldier? This would certainly have been suspected by those who knew Mary. Early rumors to this effect persisted during the first three hundred years of the Christian movement. It must have been painful for Mary and later on for Jesus to have to deal with these stories. It is not what we really are that we have to live with, but with what people around us say that we are."[25]

This last point is especially relevant to the workings of homophobia, from which no one is immune. It is not whether we are really lesbian or gay that matters to a gay basher or a military investigator or a bigoted employer or a landlord; it is what people around us say or suspect or guess or deduce from our clothes.

The book of Ruth both celebrates shockingly unconventional relationships and warns us against taking purity as the basis of our identity or of our holiness. Elizondo applies this to Jesus: "In his existence, Jesus was the antithesis of all human quests for 'purity.' "[26]

A Church Made Clean by Strangers

The main question for the early church became: Do you have to "keep kosher" to be Christian? This kind of question still bedevils us in the age of bourgeois religion: Do you have to be respectable to receive the sacraments?

Acts shows us this struggle within the early church, as well as its conclusion. Whereas the people of God called Israel were defined by kinship and by regulations of cleanliness and pollution, the people of God called Christian included polluted foreigners. This much we Christians now take for granted and feel a little smug about. But the reality of the times was a little more scandalous: these newly admitted foreigners were allowed to keep their filthy customs. Two stories from Acts still carry enough of the power of that scandal to teach us a few lessons.

Acts 10

In Acts 10 we read about Peter, who had gone on a preaching trip to the port city of Jaffa. Meanwhile, messengers from the nearby Roman headquarters of Caesarea were on their way to see Peter, sent by a generous and devout centurion named Cornelius, a "God-fearer," that is, one of a class of sympathizers with Jewish religious teachings who were not formal converts.

> About noon the next day, as [Cornelius's messengers] were on their journey and approaching the city, Peter went up on the roof to pray. He became hungry and wanted something to eat; and while it was being prepared, he fell into a trance. He saw the heaven opened and something like a large sheet coming down, being lowered to the ground by its four corners. In it were all kinds of four-footed creatures and reptiles and birds of the air. Then he heard a voice saying, "Get up, Peter; kill and eat." But Peter said, "By no means, Lord; for I have never eaten anything that is profane or unclean." The voice said to him again, a second time, "What God has made clean, you must not call profane." This happened three times [it always seems to take Peter three tries to get the message!], and the thing was suddenly taken up to heaven.
>
> Now while Peter was greatly puzzled about what to make of the vision that he had seen, suddenly the men sent by Cornelius appeared. . . . While Peter was still thinking about the vision, the Spirit said to him. "Look, three men are searching for you. Now get up, go down,

and go with them without hesitation; for I have sent them." (Acts
10:9–17, 19–20)

This last part reminds us that since Caesarea was the headquarters of
the occupying army, such a summons must have felt to Peter like
getting a visit from the FBI. Peter went to meet the messengers,
who, in due course, conducted him to Cornelius.

> On Peter's arrival Cornelius met him, and falling at his feet, worshiped
> him. But Peter made him get up, saying, "Stand up; I am only a
> mortal." And as he talked with him, he went in and found that many
> had assembled; and he said to them, "You yourselves know that it is
> unlawful for a Jew to associate with or to visit a Gentile; but God has
> shown me that I should not call anyone profane or unclean." (Acts
> 10:25–28)

Cornelius then told about a vision he had, in which he was told
to summon Peter and do whatever Peter said. Hearing this, Peter
responded, "I truly understand that God shows no partiality, but in
every nation anyone who fears [God] and does what is right is
acceptable." Peter gave a baptismal sermon; and we are told that he
was not even finished when "the Holy Spirit fell upon all who
heard the word. The circumcised believers who had come with
Peter were astounded that the gift of the Holy Spirit had been
poured out even on the Gentiles." Peter then asked the relevant
question of the hour—and of ours, as well: "Can anyone withhold
the water for baptizing these people who have received the Holy
Spirit just as we have?" (Acts 10:47). And so they were baptized.

Peter's question, in Greek, is a little convoluted and vague, but its
implication is clear: What power could stand in the way of the waters
of baptism? It sounds a little like an objection made today to the
ordination of women: you can go through all the ceremonies you
like, but when you are done, the women still are not priests because
their femaleness somehow prevents the sacrament from "taking." In
fact, the objection to baptizing Gentiles (the distinction is pointed up
in the phrase—literally, "the faithful from among the Circumcision"—that Luke uses to characterize Peter's companions) was just
this strong, and it was tearing the young movement apart, as some say
the issue of lesbians and gay men in the churches threatens to do.
Peter, we are told in Acts 11:2, was summoned to Jerusalem and
rebuked: "Some from among the Circumcision took issue with Peter,
saying, 'You entered the house of men with foreskins and ate
together with them' " (my translation). This is plain speaking—a

little plainer in the Greek than in the usual translations. Their complaint is eloquent with their disgust; they had forgotten that Jesus drank water at the hands of a Samaritan woman. Peter defended himself by recounting his dream, his summons to Caesarea, Cornelius's dream, his own sermon, and the descent of the Holy Spirit. "And I remembered the word of the Lord, how [Jesus] had said, 'John baptized with water, but you will be baptized with the Holy Spirit.' If then God gave them the same gift as [God] gave us when we believed in the Lord Jesus Christ, who was I that I could hinder God?" (Acts 11:16–17). Peter's defense ended this skirmish, though it did not lay the issue to rest.

I have emphasized the physical aspects of the distinction between clean Jews and unhygienic Gentiles because I want us to remember that this was not an abstract theological issue for the early Jesus movement. What Peter saw in his dream made his stomach turn, and what the apostles heard back in Jerusalem filled them with revulsion. You may want to pause and think of some of the foods you have heard about from other cultures that cause the same reaction in you. The presence of gay men is just as upsetting to many straight men (I cannot speak for lesbians and straight women). In fact, this gut-wrenching disgust has been offered as a justification in court by accused murderers of gay men—and accepted. There is a growing custom among those who argue against equality for lesbians and gay men of starting off by disclaiming any homophobic feelings (I suppose this is progress). The next phrase is generally some variation on "But you have to understand, this is a moral/theological/ethical/scriptural position that I'm forced, however reluctantly, to uphold." This has invaded the debate within the churches, as the debate in civil society has been poisoned by its use under the fig leaf of "Christians' rights." This more-in-sorrow-than-in-anger tone is self-delusion, if not worse. In a homophobic society, all of us are raised with homophobic value systems, just as we are raised to be racists under white supremacy. This is as true for me as it is for you.

Just so, James or Bartholomew may have said to Peter, "I don't hate uncircumcised men—but the law is clear. We can't change what Moses taught us, can we? It's not a matter of what is convenient in a cosmopolitan society but of eternal truth." The shudder of disgust at the uncut Romans' dirtiness need never have been put into words. As any honest white male Christian who has been in such places can attest, the privacy of the locker room or the exclusive men's club gives just the same permission for the raised eyebrow or the nudge of the elbow when Jews or blacks or women are mentioned.

As I said, the debate was not resolved all at once. This story represents an early dispute. In the end, Peter's view prevailed, largely because of the force of Paul's personality and missionary success. It turned out that the young movement could change what Moses taught—and did. The conclusion is clear. Not only were Cornelius and his household not required to undergo circumcision first; not only were they not instructed to eat only clean food; they were not even "washed clean" in the waters of baptism first. The Holy Spirit was manifest in them. Then came the ritual, not of washing but of death, rebirth, and incorporation into Christ's body. Clearly, they were clean enough all along.

Too many of us gay male and lesbian Christians have accepted the liturgical sequence over the scriptural one. We stand in the porch of the sanctuary, begging to be declared clean enough to come in and minister. If we look to the example given in this story, we will try a bolder strategy, proclaim the liberating acts of God in our lives, take our place among the ministers of the church, and thus show the presence of the Spirit. Then we can wait for the successors of the Apostles to catch up with God.

In time, of course, Gentiles came to outnumber Jews in the Jesus movement and this controversy became unimportant. But today, beneath the surface of some debates over declaring a congregation's openness to lesbians and gay men, a fear seems to lurk that we will similarly come to outnumber the present membership. I have heard reports of such concerns being expressed openly. The reality, of course, is that lesbians and gay men are often quite suspicious of churches' declarations of tolerance; I have seen no evidence that the declarations have slowed the tendency of gays and lesbians to give organized Christianity a wide berth.

Acts 8:26–40

A story from Acts 8:26–40 may bring the point closer to us. The apostle in this incident is Philip, who has had remarkable success among (significantly) the Samaritans. For his next assignment, an angel has directed him down the wilderness road from Jerusalem to Gaza.

> There was an Ethiopian eunuch, a court official of the Candace, queen of the Ethiopians, in charge of her entire treasury. He had come to

Jerusalem to worship and was returning home; seated in his chariot, he
was reading the prophet Isaiah. Then the Spirit said to Philip, "Go over
to this chariot and join it." So Philip ran up to it and heard him reading
the prophet Isaiah. He asked, "Do you understand what you are
reading?"

Most people in antiquity did not read silently even when alone; the
ability to do so was cause for comment throughout the Mediterranean world. So we can imagine that Philip heard the eunuch
stumbling over the foreign language, either Hebrew or, more
likely, the Greek Septuagint.

He replied, "How can I, unless someone guides me?" And he invited
Philip to get in and sit beside him. Now the passage of scripture that he
was reading was this [Isa. 53:7–8]: "Like a sheep he was led to the
slaughter, and like a lamb silent before its shearer, so he does not open
his mouth. In his humiliation justice was denied him. Who can describe
his generation? For his life is taken away from the earth." The eunuch
asked Philip, "About whom, may I ask you, does the prophet say this,
about himself or about someone else?" Then Philip began to speak, and
starting with this scripture, he proclaimed to him the good news about
Jesus."

It is a good starting point, a passage that must have struck the
eunuch deeply, with its link between being deprived of justice and
of posterity (this last is the word the NAB uses instead of "generation": "Who will tell of his posterity?"). It spoke to the eunuch's
condition so directly that he felt it was written with him in mind.
"Who is this prophet talking about?" he asked Philip.

The fact that the eunuch was reading scripture at all, of course,
gave Philip his entry; but it is significant that unlike Cornelius, this
man could never have been a full convert to Judaism, for Deut. 23:1
says, "No one whose testicles are crushed or whose penis is cut off
shall be admitted to the assembly of the LORD." Was this the
welcome the legal experts of the Temple gave the eunuch at the
end of his long and arduous journey to Jerusalem?

Deuteronomy 23, as it happens, contains two other exclusions.
Verses 17 and 18 say, "None of the daughters of Israel shall be a
temple prostitute; none of the sons of Israel shall be a temple
prostitute. You shall not bring the fee of a prostitute or the wages of
a male prostitute into the house of the LORD your God in payment
for any vow, for both of these are abhorrent to the LORD your
God" (NRSV). This is a straightforward and fairly explicit translation, but in the King James Version, beloved of many fundamental-

ists and traditionalists, we find instead a prohibition of "sodomites." This juxtaposition strengthens my own fellow feeling with the Ethiopian eunuch. Both of us are on the "wrong side" of the idea that the main goal of life is to reproduce.

But that is not all. In Deut. 23:3 we read, "No Ammonite or Moabite shall be admitted to the assembly of the LORD. Even to the tenth generation, none of their descendants shall be admitted to the assembly of the LORD." Remember that Ruth was a Moabite and that descent in Jewish law is through the mother, so David (in the third generation) was the descendant of a Moabite (Jesus was too, in the thirtieth generation). How can we continue to call "sodomites" unclean, even if it meant then what it does now?

With this background in mind, let us go on with the story in Acts: "As they were going along the road, they came to some water; and the eunuch said, 'Look, here is water! What is to prevent me from being baptized?' " (Acts 8:36). This is the same question we heard Peter ask at Cornelius's house. For a eunuch, however, it would be a real question. The lawyers had perhaps given their answer and sent him home. Something about how Philip explained Isaiah to him raised hope of a different answer this time. Perhaps Philip pointed to a passage found a few chapters later in Isa. 56:3–5, one at odds with Deuteronomy:

> Do not let the foreigner joined to the LORD say, "The LORD will surely separate me from his people"; and do not let the eunuch say, "I am just a dry tree." For thus says the LORD: To the eunuchs who keep my sabbaths, who choose the things that please me and hold fast my covenant, I will give, in my house and within my walls, a monument and a name better than sons and daughters; I will give them an everlasting name that shall not be cut off.

A monument and a name are, in Hebrew, *yad vashem:* the name of the Holocaust memorial in Jerusalem.

We will never know what the two discussed. We do know what happened next:

> [The eunuch] commanded the chariot to stop, and both of them, Philip and the eunuch, went down into the water, and Philip baptized him. When they came up out of the water, the Spirit of the Lord snatched Philip away; the eunuch saw him no more, and went on his way rejoicing. (Acts 8:38–39)

The miraculous ending sets the seal of God's favor on the encounter. The eunuch has been admitted to the people of God. The eunuch, a pilgrim to God's house, going back to a distant home perplexed and unfulfilled, meets God's love in Philip and responds with a question: Will you let someone like me in? Philip, for his part, recognizes a servant of God in this servant of the Candace. Their meeting is solemnized by baptism, by the Spirit's presence, and by rejoicing. It is as simple as that.

It is simple because Philip does not give the eunuch a list of rules to follow, does not ask a series of baptismal questions. It is the eunuch who asks questions; Philip just tells the good news of Jesus. The eunuch's perplexity is replaced by joy in the liberating power of this good news. Even if Philip did not quote Isa. 56:3–5, his good news must have been similar; much of Jesus' teaching is the same as Isaiah's. It is a message of justice for one deprived of justice; of witness by one who, speaking a foreign language, does not open his mouth; about one cut off from posterity being made a member of the body of Christ.

In Exodus, a rabble of slaves was made a new people for God. By the time of this story, Israel, although under Roman occupation, is no longer a rabble but a people with a common identity, marked off by laws such as those in Deuteronomy, laws of purity and abomination. To be a people for God, they must be able to hear again the simpler message of God's call and respond to it in love.

Theologians in Latin America, when they refer to the new people who are needed if there are to be hearers of God's Word, speak of the poor. They mean the economically poor, for an unjust system denies them justice and prevents them from speaking of their posterity, taking part in building their future, and being the agents of history. We North Americans benefit from that system. We can and must hear the voices of the poor. But notice that we have a lot in common with Cornelius and the Ethiopian finance minister. Neither of them was poor or politically powerless. They do not call forth pity, like the poor in Latin America.

Yes, we feel sorry for the eunuch: as many straight people seem to feel sorry for me, often revealing their sympathy when they ask if I am sorry that I will never have children—as they might ask a eunuch. (Unlike the eunuch, there is nothing to stop me from doing so; but if I ever do, it will not mean I am no longer gay.) But the eunuch did not feel sorry for himself. He probably would not have risen so high in the queen's household had he not been a eunuch.

Both of these converts—Cornelius and the eunuch—force us to reclaim the sense of amorality that Soelle talked about. People are not worthy because they are pitiable, any more than they are worthy because they are respectable. It is not poverty that lets these two hear, any more than destitution ennobles the poor of Latin America. It is their outsiderness, the fact that they are outcasts. They are disgusting, ritually unclean, defiled, just as we gay men are. One of them is a eunuch, the other eats unclean food. Of such is the new people of God made.

Where does that leave those who are not outcasts? That is where solidarity comes in. Remember, solidarity with lesbians and gay men is easy, since it is not, as Elizondo reminds us, what we really are but what we are thought to be that we have to make our lives from. It may be enough not to deny the rumors and speculation that will inevitably follow any public declaration in favor of lesbian and gay male liberation.

What solidarity means is the matter for chapter 5.

CHAPTER 5

In the Breaking of the Bread

After so much hatred, we yearn to love each other, and for
this reason we are the enemies of private property and the
despisers of law.

—Elisée Reclus

"Solidarity" is a word easily used but rarely defined. It may be the most important theological matter facing
Christians in the North Atlantic world, both with respect to our
relations with the exploited majority of the world, and with respect
to the divisions that have kept us from overthrowing the system of
exploitation that dominates our own countries. It is the end to
which the outward movement I have described in these chapters
tends, the final necessary element in our struggle for liberation. This
is as true for individuals as it is for social groups.

Many theologians today, explicitly or implicitly, are working to
formulate a theology of solidarity. By its nature, this is no project
for an individual. We can only do it together, sitting around the
Holy Table, bringing to life the Easter proclamation "We knew
him in the breaking of the bread."

We gather around this table for two reasons: our need for
solidarity and the needs of our bodies. I want to look at each before
turning to the events we remember in this meal.

Our Need for Each Other

Solidarity has two meanings for lesbians and gay men. First, if we
are to build that consciousness of ourselves as a class called for in
chapter 4, we will have to create solidarity among ourselves, across
the lines of gender, race, religion, and class that divide us now. This
is part of building any class consciousness, but it is especially

necessary if we hope to solve the problems we have created by seeing gayness as a "lifestyle."

I raised some of these problems earlier; first among them is the risk of fooling ourselves that we can buy ourselves out of oppression. If we are rich enough to live in New York or San Francisco, we can associate only with other gay men. If we are rich enough to own a home, we need not fear eviction by homophobic landlords. If we are rich enough, we can take all-gay cruises, vacation in all-gay resorts, and comfort ourselves with the right furnishings and clothes and habits. We can even buy a convincing facsimile of affection; we can certainly buy sexual pleasure. And the devil take the hindmost.

This is not liberation, even for individuals. It certainly is not freedom for our sisters and brothers. This is why we need politics: so we are not left to stand or fall alone.

The second problem is that we may come to rely on charismatic leaders to lead us to freedom. The popular American socialist standard-bearer Eugene Debs, warning against this hankering after a new Moses, used to say he would not lead people into the promised land even if he could, for if he could lead them in, somebody else could lead them out again. This is a recurrent danger in our political culture. Every so often we read in the gay press (not so often in the lesbian press) the lament that we have no "leadership." The American desire for instruction from experts, our love of the shortcut and the quick fix, is at the bottom of this. We would rather hire somebody to create change for us and spare ourselves the trouble.

This is why people hailed Jesus at his triumphal entry in Jerusalem. It is also why they abandoned him when they learned he was not the quick fix they expected.

We suffer from desiring instant liberation. We suffer when it does not work; we suffer more when it turns to fascism. We suffer most because it makes us responsible for the fascism it becomes. Without a full, participatory political movement, we become accomplices.[1]

Second, solidarity has to do with building ties to the political movements of other oppressed and exploited people. Without them, we will never succeed. Our failures in this line have been costly, not least because they have allowed our enemies to claim that we are asking for "special rights." Campaigns to forbid inclusion of sexual preference in civil rights legislation have succeeded with their implication that we are all male, all rich, and all white. We have felt free to appropriate the language and the demands of African Americans' struggles for civil rights, without giving anything in return. This is not the only reason some black activists speak out against making common cause with us, but we have made it easier for them to do so. Some believe that the early gay liberation movement was too quick to align itself with any vaguely progressive-sounding group, without asking for anything in return; but there are also dangers in a kind of collective go-it-alone strategy. Feminist-socialist critic Sheila Rowbotham refers to the relations between leftist women and men, but her warning applies to us as well: "We must go our own way but remember we are going to have to take them with us."[2]

Gathering around the table is a good place to think about how to build solidarity. It brings us back to our most basic bodily needs, met in the most ordinary of settings. We have noticed already that who you can eat with is a basic measure of who is outcast and who is not, who is touchable and who is not. If we are not ready to eat together, we have changed little that matters. We have changed even less if there is nothing on the table to eat.

Gathering to share a meal also tells us something about our ways of knowing. We know God and we know each other in action by sharing. A common meal does not happen by talking about it. It comes by work: not necessarily glamorous work, not necessarily even interesting work, but the kind of work we all have to do.

The liturgical heritage of the Catholic tradition is a large part of its wisdom, for the same reasons. Our worship is neither passive nor abstract. Of course, while we are gathered around this table, as around any other, we talk, we listen, we learn. But that is not what brings us together. We gather to do something.

The Needs of Our Bodies

Not all our thinking is in words. That is why liturgy is also a way of doing theology—and often a corrective to the verbal kind. We know with our bodies, just as we talk with them. In the secular world we realize this. Just look at advertising. The Protestant Reformation, in some of its branches, used to play this kind of knowledge down, but many of the heirs of the Reformation have begun to worship more liturgically in recent decades. It is now mainly Roman Catholic worship that shows a distrust for liturgy, not as a result of the restoration of the liturgy since the Second Vatican Council, as traditionalists claim, but because of a need to correct the previous lack of any intelligible speech in our liturgical practice.

Unfortunately, Catholics in the United States have internalized the accusations of superstition, anti-intellectualism, and backwardness that the Protestant majority used against us. We are ashamed of the statues and candles in our churches. Worse, we are ashamed of the little old immigrant ladies who light those candles in front of those statues. We cringe when people return from Chimayo in New Mexico or Ste. Anne de Beaupré in Quebec, telling of pilgrims approaching the sanctuaries on their knees. We protest our modernity: our religion is more modern than that.

Perhaps it is. But could it be that we are ashamed of bodily exercises in church because we are ashamed of our bodies? Could it be that we offer such strenuous bodily worship at a different altar, dedicated to Nautilus, because we believe our bodies are not good enough for the God of Abraham? In a bourgeois society, the fewer demands our work makes on our bodies, the higher our class standing. What could be clearer evidence that it is bourgeois religion that sits in the cathedra?

I need not belabor the race, sex, and class prejudices that hide beneath our embarrassment at the popular piety of our grandmothers, as they venerate the amoral Mary that Dorothee Soelle has introduced us to (see chapter 4). I certainly do not mean to suggest that all wisdom is to be found in that piety. I do suggest that such forms of piety are more honest about our bodies than the worship we offer in our statue-free suburban church buildings.

What has all this to do with gay men, you ask? Two points can be made, one regarding a prejudice and the other regarding a truth behind it. First, the prejudice: hate literature against lesbians and gay men is obsessed with our bodies and the vile things we do with them. It is the direct descendant of the titillation promised by Maria Monk and her like (see chapter 2). Fund-raising letters from the Religious Right often feature a warning against opening a sealed envelope enclosed in the mailing, because it contains shocking photographs of obscene rites at a gay pride parade. Once the sealed envelope is opened, the reader is typically confronted with a man in a dress or in leather and women with bare breasts.

What would such people think of the old religious paintings of the Madonna offering her breast to the Christ child, much less the ones where she points to his naked penis to signify that Jesus is fully human, as his aureole signifies he is fully divine? It does not matter: we do not allow such paintings in our churches anymore. The realm of the body has been relegated to the "filthy" worship of witches: a class of people rapidly and inaccurately becoming, in the Catholic Church's pronouncements, synonymous with lesbians and advocates of women's ordination.

This brings us to the truth behind the prejudice. Cast out because of our sexual desires and thereby encouraged to explore them, we have come to understand them as a way of learning about ourselves and one another. AIDS and the need to explore safer sexual practice has made our bodiliness even stronger. We share this habit of bodily knowledge with women. It is a habit that some have denounced, but as Sheila Rowbotham writes: "The manner in which we touch each other in bed is part of the way in which we learn about ourselves."[3]

How wide the cultural gap is on this issue is demonstrated by how frequently straight Christians trying to be allies confront me with worries about "promiscuity." This usually is the second or third topic in our first conversation, and it comes before I have even mentioned sex. There is no need to: from their point of view, this debate is mostly about sex and very little about justice. From mine, it is just the opposite. In many respects, sex among gay men is a triviality; if it were not, we would not get it out of the way at the outset. It is the common language of our bodies. Until we are sure the other speaks it, we are still foreigners to one another. George Chauncey devotes a chapter of his history *Gay New York* to this phenomenon, examining the bathhouses' role in forging a sense of gay community among men as early as the first decade of the twentieth century. In particular he recounts the personal friendships many men built on chance encounters there.[4] One of the things that AIDS has forced us to learn is that sexual expression does not require a genital encounter; but in a society where other kinds of touching are forbidden to men, how were we to know that until we had to figure it out?

Because we are alive to our bodies, gay men are often liturgical specialists. If liturgy is a way of teaching and learning through the senses—movement, color, texture, smell—those of us who have been forced by society to rely on a nonverbal vocabulary to find one another can be expected to master it. The "church queen" is a well-known figure, even if politeness often deprives us of our name.

This is true not only among Christians. In cultures that have constructed special niches for people who are biologically men but not socially so, such people are very often ritual specialists. The importance of ritual in our lives is shown by the fact that gay men who leave the church rarely leave the practice of ritual. They simply invent new rituals. A brilliant example of this is the Radical Faerie movement, a loose network of gay men with roots in that part of the gay liberation movement that advocated communal living, defiance of gender expectations (notably wearing clothes associated with both genders at the same time), return to the land, and exploration of neo-pagan spiritualities.

More conventional souls rose to the same challenge when faced with the need to construct rituals around the mass death brought by AIDS. Many gay men needed new rituals to avoid the painful memories that a traditional Jewish or Christian funeral might call up. Over time, circles of friends have distilled new forms for celebrating the life and mourning the passing of their brothers. It is a way of integrating new realities into a developing culture. It is also a way of claiming space for ourselves.

An authentic gay, male, Christian life, then, will be based in liturgy and in our emerging forms of popular piety. They are a room of our own from which, strengthened by long competence and free to work from our strengths, we can join others in sitting around the table of the resurrection. They are a gift we bring with us to the altar. Above all, they are our traditional theological language. We need only reclaim them, proud in the knowledge that they are by no means second best. On the contrary, liturgy and popular piety will help restore the balance upset when theological work was monopolized and thus narrowed by the ordained and the degreed.

An important case where our liturgy can correct our verbal theology is in our ideas of the resurrection. (I look at the resurrection narratives in the Bible below.) Here, we should keep in mind something the liturgy teaches us that the commentaries rarely do. Scholarly writing has sometimes presented the resurrection as a kind of final proof that Jesus was who he said he was, a magic trick that God worked as if to say, "I fooled you! He was really the second Person of the Trinity!"

By contrast, the liturgy brings out the intimate relation between the exodus and the resurrection, especially during Holy Week and at baptism. The liturgy of baptism was originally—and according to the restored Roman liturgy, is again—a central part of the liturgy of the Easter vigil. By our participation in the ceremonies of the Last

Supper, footwashing, and the cross, as in the Red Sea of baptism, we can feel the conquest of death. It emerges from the realm of speculation and becomes concrete in our ritual action, performed by our bodies.

Where Have You Taken His Body?

This connection between the exodus and the resurrection is not absent in scripture. To help us see it there more clearly, let us look at Luke 24:

> On the first day of the week, at early dawn, [the women] came to the tomb, taking the spices that they had prepared. They found the stone rolled away from the tomb, but when they went in, they did not find the body [of the Lord Jesus]. (Luke 24:1)

It is hard to find the body of the Lord Jesus in contemporary theology. We have come to despise the kind of popular devotion with which the resurrection narrative begins: practiced by women; centered on the body; expressed physically, not verbally; outside the official liturgy; and without the participation of the Apostles, the alleged models of our priesthood. The scriptural narrative promises a very different resurrection from the one mystified in books. It promises a resurrection that is the fitting complement to the incarnation.

> While they were perplexed about this, suddenly two men in dazzling clothes stood beside them. The women were terrified and bowed their faces to the ground, but the men said to them, "Why do you look for the living among the dead? He is not here, but has risen. Remember how he told you, while he was still in Galilee, that the Son of Man must be handed over to sinners, and be crucified, and on the third day rise again." Then they remembered his words, and returning from the tomb, they told all this to the eleven and to all the rest. Now it was Mary Magdalene, Joanna, Mary the mother of James, and the other women with them who told this to the apostles. But these words seemed to them an idle tale, and they did not believe them. But Peter got up and ran to the tomb; stooping and looking in, he saw the linen cloths by themselves; then he went home, amazed at what had happened. (Luke 24:4–12)

This is the first report of the resurrection. Notice that the women are the witnesses to it. This is natural: they took action, carried on with their usual, and usually ignored, women's work of caring for the bodies of the dead. The male disciples had more important work to do: figuring out how to salvage their reputations for hardheaded good sense, lost by their association with this disreputable visionary. They would go nowhere near the tomb of an executed felon; that would be fatal to recovering their respectability.

The women, I suspect, were less appalled than the men at the apparent failure of the mission. They were less tied to male ideas of what success would look like. And they had work to do: loving service to the corpse in the form of ointments and perfumes, the embalming techniques of the period. The women went to work, performed their popular devotions, and in doing so, they learned something surprising.

What they learned was not convincing to the men—a combination, no doubt, of who the witnesses were and how they learned it. Women were not considered trustworthy witnesses in court. So when they came and told an unlikely story, founded not on reason but on the mere evidence of their senses, it seemed like nonsense, and the men refused to believe it. Peter had to check for himself. Even when he saw that there was no body in the tomb, he was still perplexed. He was not yet prepared to accept the women's explanation.

This speaks to the reality of lesbians and gay men presuming to bear witness to the truth of our Christian lives. As I have said, we are not considered trustworthy witnesses. We are not "objective" enough. Like other oppressed people, we are presumed not to be able to read for ourselves. Only those with power to keep are supposed to be objective enough to make judgments about scripture. The rest of us are supposed to be so biased, so lacking in credentials, that we can never understand the true meaning of scripture. When we try to report what we have seen (especially if our experience points away from official truth) or, worse, offer explanations, we are dismissed.

All liberation theologies are founded on the need to break down these suppositions, first of all by pointing out that the ones supposed to be objective are, in fact, the ones who have power that they would prefer to enjoy unmolested. The rest of us can take comfort in the fact that the first witnesses of the resurrection were not believed either. But what they reported turned out to be true.

This should not surprise us; the women at the tomb were the best hearers all along. Luke tells us that Jesus' words came back to them: "Ah, yes. He always told us it was going to end this way." If they did not find this hard to accept, it was because they had been listening to what Jesus really said, while the ones with power, including the men among the disciples, had only been listening to see if their own expectations would be met. Remember all the times the disciples discussed what Jesus meant instead of doing anything—for instance, who would get to sit on the right-hand side of Jesus' throne when he became king. True disciples, by contrast, act on what they hear.

Why should such true discipleship be so frequently the province of outcasts, as it seems to be in the Gospels? Maybe it is simply because not doing anything is a guarantee of continued oppression, a guarantee that nothing will change. Maybe that is why insiders prefer to talk instead.

The Meanings of Intimacy

It is not as if the insiders at the resurrection did not have clear teaching. They had, after all, the raising of Lazarus. John 11:1–44 tells us:

> Now a certain man was ill, Lazarus of Bethany, the village of Mary and her sister Martha. Mary was the one who anointed the Lord with perfume and wiped his feet with her hair; her brother Lazarus was ill. So the sisters sent a message to Jesus, "Lord, he whom you love is ill." But when Jesus heard it, he said, "This illness does not lead to death; rather it is for God's glory, so that the Son of God may be glorified through it." Accordingly, though Jesus loved Martha and her sister and Lazarus, after having heard that Lazarus was ill, he stayed two days longer in the place where he was.
>
> Then after this he said to the disciples, "Let us go to Judea again." (John 11:1–7)

The disciples object, because of the hostility and danger that they will encounter there; but Jesus insists: "Our friend Lazarus has fallen asleep, but I am going there to awaken him" (11:11). The disciples misunderstand, until finally "Jesus told them plainly, 'Lazarus is dead' " (11:14).

> When Jesus arrived, he found that Lazarus had already been in the tomb four days. . . . When Martha heard that Jesus was coming, she went and met him, while Mary stayed at home. Martha said to Jesus, "Lord, if you had been here, my brother would not have died. But even now I know that God will give you whatever you ask. . . ." Jesus said to her, "Your

brother will rise again." Martha said to him, "I know that he will rise again in the resurrection on the last day." Jesus said to her, "I am the resurrection and the life. Those who believe in me, even though they die, will live, and everyone who lives and believes in me will never die. Do you believe this?" She said to him, "Yes, Lord, I believe that you are the Messiah, the Son of God, the one coming into the world." (John 11:17, 20–27)

Then Martha brings Mary, who repeats Martha's reproach.

When Jesus saw her weeping, and the Jews who came with her also weeping, he was greatly disturbed in spirit and deeply moved. He said, "Where have you laid him?" They said to him, "Lord, come and see." Jesus began to weep. So the Jews said, "See how he loved him!" But some of them said, "Could not he who opened the eyes of the blind man have kept this man from dying?"

Then Jesus, again greatly disturbed, came to the tomb. It was a cave, and a stone was lying against it. Jesus said, "Take away the stone." (John 11:33–39)

Martha warned him of the smell of corruption—perhaps they were too poor to afford the kinds of spices and perfumes that the women brought to Jesus' tomb—but they proceed, and Jesus prays aloud. Then,

he cried with a loud voice, "Lazarus, come out!" The dead man came out, his hands and feet bound with strips of cloth, and his face wrapped in a cloth. Jesus said to them, "Unbind him, and let him go." (John 11:43–44)

John tells this story, shortly before the final entry into Jerusalem, to teach about Jesus' divinity; it is meant to foreshadow the resurrection. But why this particular foreshadowing? The raising of Lazarus not only shows that Jesus has power. It shows that we literally cannot live without one another. Today we may read Jesus' expression of love for Lazarus as some kind of Middle Eastern demonstrativeness; but John tells us the onlookers remarked on it.

Emotional connections are not enough in themselves. At the crucial junctures in our lives, we need a bodily presence to make the connections clear. We experience and understand love through our bodies: "If you had been here, my brother would not have died," Martha tells Jesus, and in case we do not get the point, John has Mary use the very same words.

John's depiction of Jesus catechizing Martha about the doctrine of the resurrection, which at first reading seems a bit heavy-handed, only reinforces this idea. Martha knows that she can ask Jesus to perform a miracle; but, practical as always, she does it only after first pointing out that if Jesus had come when called, no miracle would have been necessary. His bodily presence would have been enough. Lazarus would have lived, because he would have been able to feel again the bond of love between them.

This idea is not strange to us. It is why we hold hands with suffering people whom we love, even when they are unconscious. This story merely takes the idea a step further: once this bodily presence, the "sacrament" of the bond of love, is restored, Lazarus's life is restored, in a moment of unbinding and setting free. Not only love but embodied love is the power that conquers death.

Friendship and love bear an untidy and, in our society, uneasy relation to each other. Our bodies get in our way. We cannot deny them, since without them we cannot feel. But we want to deny them because we have never learned to be comfortable in them. This is especially true of men, who are expected to sacrifice their bodies to work and to war. It is one reason why friendships between men are so difficult. The potential of homosexuality seems always to lurk in the shadows. This is one of the ways in which homophobia diminishes all of us, gay or not.

So the story of Lazarus's raising embarrasses us. Yet if we are to understand the mystery of the resurrection, if we are to perceive the common theme in the stories of the Risen One's appearance to his friends, we must look hard at the untidiness of our passions for one another. This is a theological task in its own right, but it is one with a special relevance to theologizing about gayness. We live in a country that is obsessed by sex, and that obsession is often used to understand or explain or attack lesbians and gay men. Sex, it is then assumed, is all we are about. (By way of compensation, lesbians and gay men sometimes insist that sex has nothing to do with who we are. But we are human beings, nothing more or less.) In the end, lesbians and gay men seem to speak a different language from that of straight people, and vice versa.

A good example of the mutual incomprehension arising from different conceptions of sex is the furor surrounding Blanche Wiesen Cook's recent biography of Eleanor Roosevelt.[5] Many of us see the biography's exploration of her close relations with a variety of women, some of them openly lesbian, as revealing a new dimension of tenderness and humanity in an already beloved figure. There seem to be (if we believe Wiesen Cook) some straight people who see the same discussion as besmirching the name of a great American who is no longer around to defend herself. To connect these friendships with "homosexuality" in any way, they claim, is to overgeneralize and to drain the term of any meaningful content.

From my perspective as a gay man, there are several weaknesses to this argument. Most basic is the fact that most of us regard "homosexuality" as the imposition of false categories on us that do not mesh with our actual lives. It is why we do not use the word: "homosexual" is the oppressor's name for us, not ours. Why should we care if it loses its meaning?

The reason we object to the word "homosexual" reveals the next weakness in this overprotective approach to history: the implication that lesbian or gay male relations are first and foremost sexual, while heterosexual relations are not. In the case of figures from the past, our recognition of affinity with them is assumed to be tantamount to a claim that they engaged in homosexual genital activity. We feel no need to prove any such thing. It is the emotional connection, the loving relations, that draw us to them. Recall Bernard and Malachy (see the Introduction). I have no reason to doubt that they were true to their vows of celibacy. I would say the same about the relations between Edmund of Canterbury and his chancellor Richard, later bishop of Chichester (though Richard refused to take holy orders as long as Edmund was alive); or about the relations between Aelred and his monks (though what may have happened at the court of King David of Scotland before Aelred became a Cistercian monk is another matter).

No lesbian or gay man denies that we are capable of celibacy, though many who object to our ordination or to our presence in the armed forces, to name only two issues, do deny it. We deny only that celibacy is a universal precondition for us to live a Christian life. The usual reply to this position is that in advocating that homosexual and heterosexual practice be put on a basis of parity, we overemphasize sex and demean the value of chastity. The liberal version of this is to say that sex should be private and that our insistence on acknowledging its importance gives it undue prominence. Just keep quiet about it and all will be well.

But segregating sex from "proper" topics of discussion renders it far more important than simply acknowledging it as an aspect of human behavior. Thinking about the nature of certain of Eleanor Roosevelt's friendships or wondering what might have transpired between George Washington and Alexander Hamilton has the effect, over time, of restoring sex to its proper place as one of many elements, along with political sympathy or artistic taste, for example, of that extraordinarily complex and fascinating occurrence, a connection between two human beings. That, in turn, might allow us to think about, for instance, the role of presidents' wives, in ways that go beyond the two boxes we have forced them into up to now: gracious hostess or evil puppet-mistress.

Still, raising such possibilities has the effect, for many people, of casting a shadow of suspicion over otherwise perfectly innocent friendships. We might ask, just because a friendship is ostensibly without sexual content, does that mean it is "innocent"—as if such friendships never lead to perfectly wicked behavior, such as acquaintance rape? Does not defining "innocent" that way imply that any sexual relations between two women or two men are "guilty"? Responding with such questions, however reasonable they may seem, does little to remove the anxiety that many people feel over friendships now that their homosexual potential is no longer safely out of the question. However comfortable the parties may be, there remains the question of what others, all of them brought up in a homophobic culture, will think.

Our meditations on the intimacy between Jesus and Lazarus, Bernard and Malachy, or Richard and Edmund may be helpful in this matter. Notice that the approach is not the superficially attractive "Who cares what people will think?" Jesus cared deeply what people thought. Bernard cared even more, if that is possible. We may say it is what they cared about most—because they believed that what most people think is often wrong, especially when what people think leads them to cast others out on the basis of not personal character but impersonal characteristics.

As I have mentioned before, it is no accident that the saints I have named all lived in a Cistercian atmosphere. Malachy was not a Cistercian, but he died wearing the habit, as a guest at Clairvaux. Edmund died wearing it as a refugee at another Cistercian house, Pontigny, and Richard lived the Cistercian life with him there. Another Cistercian, Aelred, seems to have been led to take the habit in part by the example of the dearest friend of his youth, Waldef, King David of Scotland's stepson. Waldef ended up as abbot of yet another Cistercian abbey, Melrose.

Of all these, Aelred wrote the most about the importance of intimate friendships in developing a rounded spiritual life, the purpose of a monastery. It is worth noting that he permitted physical affection between his monks. Douglass Roby, in an introduction to Aelred's *Spiritual Friendship,* comments:

> There may well have been a homosexual component to his youthful friendship which he found very disturbing, even if he was not fully aware of its implications. . . . The later evidence of Aelred's life would seem to indicate, however, that if this was the case, Aelred suffered no emotional damage from the experience. The close and very emotional friendships which he was able to enjoy in the monastery prove that a negative reaction to his own youthful crush on a member of the court of Scotland [Waldef, the king's stepson?] did not inhibit his emotional freedom in later life. It is also interesting to remember that Walter Daniel [Aelred's nurse and biographer] specifically noted that Aelred, unlike some other abbots, was not scandalized by demonstrations of affection, such as holding hands, by his monks. Aelred, in other words, seems to have had not only confidence in his own ability to deal with the sexual component of his friendships, but to have trusted his monks to be able to do the same. Nor is there any evidence that Aelred's confidence was misplaced.[6]

This atmosphere is consistent with the heteroeroticism expressed in the Cistercian's devotion to Mary. (The awkwardness of the word "heteroeroticism" is interesting. When we compare it to the ease with which even members of Congress can pronounce "homoeroticism," we discover something of how privileged the language of the dominators is.) This Cistercian devotion had a strong link to the tradition of courtly love. It was encouraged by these monks vowed to chastity, because they had a principle for distinguishing good eroticism from bad: *cupiditas,* which Aelred, among others, described as a love that seeks only the self's good, not the beloved's. For Aelred, that critical principle was as sound in judging monastic friendships as any other kind.

I do not assume that these friendships mean that Aelred or any of his monks were "homosexuals." If we accept the constructionist position, even with reservations, we will be inclined to avoid calling people "homosexuals" before the medical model underlying the word could have been part of their self-understanding. At the same time, gay historian, playwright, and activist Martin Duberman suggests that such historical figures, "who escaped compulsory heterosexuality in any of the limited number of ways available in a given time period—for example, entering a convent (or monastery) to escape pressure to marry—can appropriately be claimed as having been at least 'proto-gay'."[7]

In the end, though, it is irrelevant whether any of these medieval saints were "homosexuals." We look to their lives as models for contemporary action. We make saints for the same reason, as the poor of Central America have done with Archbishop Romero. Where their lives and example seem to offer guidance in the concrete situation of our lives, at a time when the category "gay" does exist, we are right to draw on that guidance.

The lives of the saints are simply materials we gay men can use to figure out how to express our lives and our friendships toward one another. Like other lay people, we are hampered by the fact that so many official saints are priests, monks, nuns, or otherwise vowed to celibacy. The few lay people who are canonized are married—and their sexual activity, though permitted, was often "sacrificed," if we believe the tales—or specifically described as virgins. We need to raise up saints of our own choosing to supplement the official ones. But the example even of officially recognized saints indicates that strong attachments, even the "particular friendships" we have so often been warned against, do not prevent sanctity. They may even cause it.

It is quite possible, by the way, for a perfectly sound friendship of the kind Aelred praised to exist between a gay man and a straight one. They are unfortunately rare, but I can count a few in my own life. Some have not even required any uncommon exertions from either of us. The (married) dedicatee of this book, for instance, has been gifted all along with the vision to see a relatively uncommon intimacy between us, including holding hands in public like Aelred's monks, as natural—more so than I have, usually, but then he is younger and wiser. I have been told that there are friendships between straight men and women that manage to survive a sexual attraction felt by only one party. Because we have developed social forms to guide us in such cases, we do not think about them much.

Recognizing the Risen One

Social forms set Luke 24:13–53, the next scene of Luke's resurrection story, in motion:

> [Later that same day, two disciples] were going to a village called Emmaus, about seven miles from Jerusalem, and talking with each other about all these things that had happened. While they were talking and discussing, Jesus himself came near and went with them, but their

eyes were kept from recognizing him. And he said to them, "What are you discussing with each other while you walk along?" . . . Then one of them, whose name was Cleopas, answered him, "Are you the only stranger in Jerusalem who does not know the things that have taken place there in these days?" He asked them, "What things?" They replied, "The things about Jesus of Nazareth, who was a prophet mighty in deed and word before God and all the people, and how our chief priests and leaders handed him over to be condemned to death and crucified him. But we had hoped that he was the one to redeem Israel. Yes, and besides all this, it is now the third day since these things took place. Moreover, some women of our group astounded us. They were at the tomb early this morning, and when they did not find his body there, they came back and told us that they had indeed seen a vision of angels who said that he was alive. Some of those who were with us went to the tomb and found it just as the women had said; but they did not see him." Then he said to them, "Oh, how foolish you are, and how slow of heart to believe all that the prophets have declared! Was it not necessary that the Messiah should suffer these things and then enter into his glory?" Then beginning with Moses and all the prophets, he interpreted to them the things about himself in all the scriptures.

As they came near the village to which they were going, he walked ahead as if he were going on. But they urged him strongly, saying, "Stay with us, because it is almost evening and the day is now nearly over." So he went in to stay with them. When he was at the table with them, he took bread, blessed and broke it, and gave it to them. Then their eyes were opened, and they recognized him; and he vanished from their sight. They said to each other, "Were not our hearts burning within us while he was talking to us on the road, while he was opening the scriptures to us?" That same hour they got up and returned to Jerusalem; and they found the eleven and their companions gathered together. They were saying, "The Lord has risen indeed, and he has appeared to Simon!"[8] Then they told what had happened on the road, and how he had been made known to them in the breaking of the bread. (Luke 24:13–35)

How did they come to know Jesus there and not before? In other words, what is the nature of true understanding? We may start by looking at what fails to bring understanding. There are two steps in the process. First, Jesus' companionship and support in their bereavement does not lead them to understand. We may not be able to live without one another, but love does not guarantee understanding; nor does explanation. Jesus tells the whole story, but at first his words do not enlighten them.

Then comes the second step. When they have responded to his words by offering hospitality, according to the social forms, Jesus breaks bread with them. Then they recognize him. Jesus has taken the social form, the "choreography" (to use Monika Hellwig's term), and lifted it to another level. It begins with convention. It ends with transformation. This progression mirrors the movement we have examined in the previous chapters. There is first the acknowledgment of kinship—coming out. Then there is sharing of our experiences—consciousness raising. But true understanding comes in action taken together, as a gathered people, which is what "liturgy" literally means.

Reciprocity is at the heart of this. Cleopas and his friend do not understand by listening and discussing. They do understand by offering hospitality, an opening to the stranger, which Jesus then accepts. He breaks bread, and they can hear. Both parties show mercy: Cleopas and his friends offer a place to stay. Jesus breaks the bread he has brought. And both parties share the joy. They are so excited that they have to go all the way back to Jerusalem right then and tell the others what has happened.

According to Mark 11:13, their report was not believed at first. Luke's tale continues:

> While they were talking about this, Jesus himself stood among them and said to them, "Peace be with you." They were startled and terrified, and thought that they were seeing a ghost. He said to them, "Why are you frightened, and why do doubts arise in your hearts? Look at my hands and my feet; see that it is I myself. Touch me and see; for a ghost does not have flesh and bones as you see that I have." And when he had said this, he showed them his hands and his feet. While in their joy they were disbelieving and still wondering, he said to them, "Have you anything here to eat?" They gave him a piece of broiled fish, and he took it and ate in their presence.
>
> Then he said to them, "These are my words that I spoke to you while I was still with you—that everything written about me in the law of Moses, the prophets, and the psalms must be fulfilled." Then he opened their minds to understand the scriptures. (Luke 24:36–45)

Again we have the breaking of bread—or in this case, fish—followed by understanding the message of scripture. The order is becoming typical, which suggests that there is a message in the order itself. By remembering how, in chapter 4, I showed that admittance to the table defines "in groups" by creating "out groups," we can make sense of this. Remember that, according to John 20:19, the disciples had locked themselves in. Still Jesus got in. Locking ourselves in never helps us; but until Jesus is among us, nothing makes sense. Unless we have an open table, one from which no one is barred as unclean, we can never hope to grasp what Jesus is teaching us. (This is the reverse of our liturgical order of celebrating the Holy Supper, which is talk first, food after.)

Moreover, it is when the Emmaus travelers tell their story to the rest that Jesus comes in. This recalls what I said about the importance of telling our stories publicly and naming our oppression. Here it is how the gathered disciples make Jesus present. The gathering is important. Remembering our stories by ourselves and hoarding our grievances in secret while outwardly trying to pass are not acts of liberation. Sharing our experiences in the midst of the assembly brings Jesus among us. This liturgical occasion in Luke brings us into the heart of God's love, because the disciples are telling the story of one they love. By naming the beloved, the beloved appears. The power of love incarnates the beloved, as the presence of the lover brought Lazarus back from death.

In the context of Luke's narrative, this story is an opening out of the meal in Emmaus: the private encounter in the village becomes the public worship—the liturgy in the fullest sense—in the city. It demonstrates once more the intimate bonds between word and act, between teaching and service, between reflection and action.

It also reminds us, from a different perspective than John's story of the raising of Lazarus, that Jesus' body is not peripheral to who he is. His body can be touched, can eat food and share food with others. One of the most persistent heresies, found even among otherwise impeccably orthodox Christian theologians, is the tendency to think of the body as impure and the spirit as pure. This point of view may have arisen from Greek influences; but it persists because of our preoccupation with dividing the pure and the impure, our desire to feel clean by denouncing someone else as unclean.

We feel safer when we spiritualize, disembody, the message of the gospel. Those of us who benefit from the present allotment of resources can then claim that liberation is purely spiritual, that feeding the hungry only means giving spiritual food to the spiritually hungry, that giving shelter is going to church together.

But Jesus has a body and eats, even in the resurrection, and he tells us to touch it. We cannot spirit God's body away to avoid the political implications of the incarnation, and we cannot avoid it because we feel squeamish about one man touching another. We must face Jesus' body. Only then, when we have touched his body and eaten with him, can we theologize. And we must theologize. Something we cannot explain is happening here, after all, right in the midst of our daily existence. Somebody we buried is here eating fish and saying, "Touch me." What can this mean?

Jesus shows the way: "Remember," he told them, "I was telling you this the other day." Luke conveys a strong feeling of friends gathered; Jesus seems to have been taking up where he left off last time. "Then he opened their minds to understand the scriptures" (24:45). Now they could hear what he told them; the testimony they had discounted, because they distrusted female witnesses and small-town witnesses, had turned out to be true. The witness of the outcast was vindicated. Now they understood the relational nature of gospel knowing, in the breaking of the bread, in the sharing of the fish. In eating together, in touching, in sharing the acts of our bodies with one another, we understand.

Now they were ready for Jesus' last preaching:

> Thus it is written, that the Messiah is to suffer and to rise from the dead on the third day, and that repentance [*metanoia*] and forgiveness of sins is to be proclaimed in his name to all nations, beginning from Jerusalem. You are witnesses of these things. And see, I am sending upon you what my Father promised; so stay here in the city until you have been clothed with power from on high. (Luke 24:46–49)

Notice that word *metanoia*. It means they are to preach that the old ways of thinking and knowing are obsolete. This is not remorse or hair-shirt penance. It is getting rid of the old mental habits that keep us enslaved. It is starting all over, setting out on the road to liberation. *Metanoia* means doing what we have been trying to do in this book.

> Then he led them out as far as Bethany [where he raised Lazarus], and, lifting up his hands, he blessed them. While he was blessing them, he withdrew from them and was carried up into heaven. And they worshiped him, and returned to Jerusalem with great joy; and they were continually in the temple blessing God. (Luke 24:50–53)

The gathered followers of Jesus are finally ready for his departure. Without these surrounding events, the resurrection cannot make sense. The witness of the women, the encounter on the road to Emmaus, the meeting and sharing of food and talk are all parts of the resurrection story. Jesus' followers can bear his departure because now they know that his resurrection is not just poetic but bodily. They touched his body, and now they know how to make it present forever: by telling the story, by eating together, and by going out of their locked room into the world. They can do these things to bring Jesus back, but they can do them only as a group. None of these acts is completely solitary. Even preaching is not; it requires listeners. Salvation is not personal but communal.

Now that they understand, they are ready for the first time to become a community of lovers, something they could not do while Jesus was still teaching among them. They could not because, as we saw before, they either expected to do it all by themselves, like Judas, or they expected Jesus to do it all for them, like those who hailed him as king. Now they can build a community of love, beginning with preparing like good Jews for the Feast of Pentecost, when they will become a new kind of Christian family.

Christ's resurrection is therefore completed in community. This is the meaning of the appearance narratives in all four Gospels: proof not that the resurrection was true but of the social dimension of the resurrection itself.

Opening the Circle

In John 21, we have another meal, this time in Galilee, the place where the disciples were originally called together:

> Gathered there together were Simon Peter, Thomas called the Twin, Nathanael of Cana in Galilee, the sons of Zebedee, and two others of his disciples. Simon Peter said to them, "I am going fishing." They said to him, "We will go with you." They went out and got into the boat, but that night they caught nothing.
>
> Just after daybreak, Jesus stood on the beach; but the disciples did not know that it was Jesus. Jesus said to them, "Children, you have no fish, have you?" They answered him, "No." He said to them, "Cast the net to the right side of the boat, and you will find some." So they cast it, and now they were not able to haul it in because there were so many fish. That disciple whom Jesus loved said to Peter, "It is the Lord!" When Simon Peter heard that it was the Lord, he put on some clothes, for he was naked, and jumped into the sea. (John 21:2–7)

This seems typical of Peter. Most people take their clothes off before they jump in the water; Peter puts his on and then jumps in. It is typical also of his enthusiasm. We will see how Jesus uses his loving impulses in a moment.

> When they had gone ashore, they saw a charcoal fire there, with fish on it, and bread. Jesus said to them, "Bring some of the fish that you have just caught." So Simon Peter went aboard and hauled the net ashore,

full of large fish, a hundred fifty-three of them; and though there were so many, the net was not torn. Jesus said to them, "Come and have breakfast." Now none of the disciples dared to ask him, "Who are you?" because they knew it was the Lord. Jesus came and took the bread and gave it to them, and did the same with the fish. This was now the third time that Jesus appeared to the disciples after he was raised from the dead.

When they had finished breakfast, Jesus said to Simon Peter, "Simon son of John, do you love me more than these?" He said to him, "Yes, Lord, you know that I love you." Jesus said to him, "Feed my lambs." A second time he said to him, "Simon son of John, do you love me?" He said to him, "Yes, Lord, you know that I love you." Jesus said to him, "Tend my sheep." He said to him the third time, "Do you love me?" And he said to him, "Lord, you know everything; you know that I love you." Jesus said to him, "Feed my sheep. Very truly, I tell you, when you were younger, you used to fasten your own belt and to go wherever you wished. But when you grow old, you will stretch out your hands, and someone else will fasten a belt around you and take you where you do not wish to go." (John 21:9–18)

And then the disciples squabbled once more over who was Jesus' favorite.

This story has many elements in common with Luke's scene on the road to Emmaus. Both tell of hospitality: the sharing of food, the breaking of bread. They teach the same lesson: Jesus is made known in familiar acts. The disciples in John 21 have gone back to their former work in Galilee. Unlike Luke, John offers no suggestion of a movement or a community in formation. The Jesus story is over. The resurrection story, although they have seen the Risen One, has not yet begun.

It begins here. As in the Emmaus story, the disciples have plenty of opportunities to know who Jesus is—this is not even his first appearance to them—but they fail to recognize him until he gives them some practical help fishing. Meanwhile, Jesus does the ordinary work of community: starting the fire, setting out the bread, cooking the fish. The bread and fish remind us of the story of the loaves and fishes and of our duty to share our food as long as there are hungry people to feed.

In the scene that follows, John opens out this shared meal beyond the closed circle on the lakeshore, just as Luke opened it from the three people in Emmaus to the whole gathering of disciples in Jerusalem. Jesus' question to Peter, repeated three times—"Do you love me?"—is often used by Catholics to show Jesus giving his power to the church and particularly the hierarchy, represented by Peter. But John depicts Peter here as even slower than usual. In any case, John's Gospel offers a countervision to the hierarchical church based on the Twelve that is hinted at in the other three gospels. If this passage teaches us anything about that church, it is that its members are so ashamed of the naked body that they get fully dressed to go swimming.

So what is this scene really about? How does it move beyond the "in-group" on the beach? Why does Jesus ask the question three times? The answer is in Peter's reaction. He loses his temper: "Well, you know everything, Jesus, what are you getting at? Sure I love you." Jesus just repeats, "Feed my sheep." If you love me, do not just say so, do something. I'm giving you a chance to make up for denying me three times, by pledging your love to me three times. I'm forgiving your denial, but my kind of forgiveness is about repairing broken friendships. It is not about taking power and wearing a tiara in the Vatican (and the ensuing argument over Jesus' favoritism for John is a way of bringing this point home).

How do we repair broken friendships? Not by words alone. Peter must accept the love Jesus offers and spread it around. Loaves and fishes. "Feed my lambs. Tend my sheep. Feed my sheep."

The tone of this gathering, like the one at Emmaus, is intimate. Here they are, back in Galilee, back on that lake where they spent so much of their time together, back just trying to make a living fishing—nothing glamorous. Jesus offers some friendly advice, the way one fisherman will do for another. Then they all have a fish fry on the beach. Just as telling their story on the road brings Jesus back into Cleopas's and his friend's lives, the sharing of these fish, the loving communion of Jesus' companions—literally, here, the ones who share bread with Jesus—brings him into their midst.

The Knowings of Liturgy

Bringing Jesus into our lives happens in the breaking of the bread. Ultimately, we know Jesus not through theology but through liturgy. What does it mean, then, that so many liturgical specialists in the modern church are gay men? There is a common, if slightly bitter, joke among gay male Christians about the quickest way to get some respect for our work in the church. Imagine next Sunday morning. All over the world, in different ways, Christians are gathered for worship. The hubbub of fellowship gives way to an expectant silence as people wait for the service to begin. But by some miracle, all of the gay men have been carried away, just for this morning. Organists vanish from their benches, singers from their choir lofts. Readers, preachers, priests, and altar servers—even an occasional bishop—are nowhere to be found. What would happen next?

I suppose, were the situation to continue, one thing that would happen in the Catholic Church would be the ordination of women. But leaving aside the matter of filling the vacancies thus created, what would it mean to have no liturgical specialists? In a North Atlantic culture that values only the word as a means of communication, we may think it would not make much difference. We live in a period, after all, when we Catholics are rapidly destroying our liturgical life. I have already suggested that there is a connection between this hostility to liturgy and hostility to our bodies.

But more is at stake here. Liturgy, as I noted, is one of the ways we teach and learn about our faith. The word "orthodoxy" is ambiguous in its native Greek. It can mean not only "straight teaching" but, since *doxa* means praise, "right worship." For people who have been excluded, for one reason or another, from the formal credentials required to be straight teachers, acts of worship are our teaching medium. That medium can take various forms. It may be the home altar in a Puerto Rican housewife's bedroom. It may be the fellowship among the altar-guild ladies while they iron surplices and polish the Communion silver. Or—and this is where gay men have particularly flourished—it may be the praise offered from the musicians' gallery. All these are ways of making our voices heard when we are expected to keep silence. The liturgy, reformed or unreformed, is in the hands of the laity, whatever the clergy may think. That is what the Greek word *leitourgia* means: the work of the people, as opposed to the sacrifices of a pagan priesthood. We know Jesus not in the ordination of the priests but in the breaking of the bread—something that no priest may perform without the presence of the people.

We know Jesus three ways in the breaking of the bread. One is in the promise of future communion in the end time. Jesus breaks bread with his gathered disciples before he scatters them. There is an ancient liturgical prayer—one of the oldest we still have, from the *Didache*—that teaches with the power of poetry: "Just as this one bread which we break, once scattered over the hills, has been gathered and made one, so may thy Church too be assembled from the ends of the earth in thy kingdom!"[9] As the disciples go out to spread the good news, the breaking of the bread preserves their sense of community.

This community extends through the generations. That is an important aspect of liturgy, one little appreciated in today's world of instant solutions. The elements that keep communicating endure. The ones that do not drop away.

By this process, liturgy becomes a sign of the communion of saints. I have mentioned a few saints whom gay men can look to for guidance on the road to liberation. There may be other people in Christian history, remote or recent, who are candidates for popular canonization. We need to commemorate their lives, draw on other sources, and create a cycle of honor and remembrance through the liturgical year. We need to develop a calendar. The church's calendar is a liturgical sanctification of time. Developing our own calendar will keep us rooted in time and remind us that we are products of history.

We have started a secular calendar. In the United States, we celebrate the Stonewall Rebellion in June. We are learning to observe Coming Out Day on October 11; by origin, this is an annual commemoration of the 1987 March on Washington. Perhaps we will find another way to celebrate the 1993 March on Washington on April 25. We would do well to remember the looting and burning by the Nazis of Magnus Hirschfeld's Institute for Sexual Science on May 6, 1933; the assassination of San Francisco supervisor Harvey Milk on November 27, 1978; or (in the United States) the founding of the Society for Human Rights in Chicago on November 9, 1924. A gay male holiday with a long popular history is Halloween. Once it was the only day when men could dress as women in public without risking arrest. Historian George Chauncey describes a New York variation of this tradition from the early part of the twentieth century. It grew out of a more general Thanksgiving custom among poorer New Yorkers, "ragamuffin parades" similar to trick-or-treating on Halloween. "By holding an annual drag ball on Thanksgiving, gay men both built on the day's tradition of masquerade and expanded the inversion it implied. On a day that celebrated the family, they assembled to celebrate their membership in a gay family."[10]

To these, gay male Christians may add saints' days: Aelred on March 3, Richard on April 3, Waldef on August 3, Malachy on November 3. (Perhaps providence was giving us a hint by calling them home in such a tidy pattern?) Bernard's feast is August 20; Edmund's is November 16. From the Eastern churches comes the feast of the martyrs Sergius and Bacchus, whose blessing is called down on the two men joined in "spiritual brotherhood" in the liturgy John Boswell describes in *Rediscovering Gay History*,[11] and at greater length in his recent *Same-Sex Unions in Premodern Europe*. In the latter he describes and translates a number of liturgical texts for such unions; there are reports that some of these rites are already being used again in this country. (According to Boswell, it was customary in the Balkans, as recently as the beginning of the twentieth century, to perform these ceremonies on the Feast of St. John—December 27 in the Roman rite.)[12] More familiar and more defiant is Joan the Maid, whose feast day is May 30, the day she was burned as a heretic after resuming her wearing of men's clothing.[13] We may want to think of other traditional feast days and their special importance to us. For example, as we grapple with the losses of so many lovers and friends to AIDS, we can draw strength from Mexican popular traditions for All Souls Day. We may want to adopt the Russian custom of celebrating Holy Trinity as the feast of love and reconciliation or adopt the Byzantine feasts of the Raising of Lazarus (the Saturday before Palm Sunday) and the Samaritan Woman (fourth Sunday of Easter). We may want to recapture some of the religious meaning of a holiday we have long celebrated, Mardi Gras. We may want to develop richer forms of celebrating the incarnation, especially since the year-end holidays can be hard for those of us estranged from birth families.

It is important to reclaim our churches' traditions and give them meanings that are rooted in our lives. We must beware of becoming a sect, for that is the opposite of solidarity. Although we have been expelled from some churches, we must not excommunicate them in return. The liturgical life of Dignity groups and Protestant congregations that have seceded or been thrown out of their denominations must look to the stories of Esther and Ruth, the exiles who save because of their situations of estrangement, not in spite of them.

Our exile is one of our tools; it offers us the critical distance that we need to resurrect the whole church. We only impoverish ourselves if we try to avoid this rebuilding by adding new sect walls. What we said about solidarity above is true here as well: it can save us from becoming accomplices in oppression. We also impoverish ourselves if we see our exile as permanent. We must pray to be gathered like the scattered seed, so that we can offer our gifts at the altar alongside our sisters and brothers.

For gathering is the second meaning in the breaking of the

bread. After we have been scattered, after we have done our work of ministry, the Holy Table brings us back together. The work may not be complete, but it must be begun. Jesus is present in the breaking of the bread because it is a sign of the commonwealth, where all are fed and none is hungry and where all are agents, all are subjects of history, in charge of their own destiny. In the commonwealth, we can all do our own fishing.

Most of all, Jesus is among us in the breaking of bread when we are no longer victims. In the resurrection we are made free of death. That means we are free too of the little deaths our oppressors try to inflict on us. We may not have much power, but we do have the power to refuse to be victims any longer, to trust instead that all deaths have been swallowed up in the victory of the cross. All will be fed and the commonwealth is at hand not when the powerful hand down crumbs but when we act in solidarity. The Holy Table is the model for this action. We can break bread among ourselves. We can tell stories among ourselves. We can go fishing.

Third, in the common action of breaking bread, Jesus teaches us to know and understand. In this thanksgiving action (to borrow the Spanish phrase for Mass, *acción de gracias*), which is liturgy in its basic sense, we open our circles, just as the resurrection celebrations opened from smaller groups to larger. Because Jesus is present in the breaking of the bread, we have the means to build the loving community. This was the ingredient missing before the resurrection. The breaking of the bread is how we continue the resurrection, which (the liturgy itself teaches us) continues the liberating act of exodus. Without these, the community cannot hold together.

But Jesus does not build the community for us. Building it is our part of the liturgy. And that presents us with still more questions.

CHAPTER 6

One Bread, One Body

We are all fairies down to the feet.
—W. S. Gilbert, *Iolanthe*

Any theology rooted in life will always generate new questions. I have not tried to answer all the questions facing us now, only suggested the general trajectory of an authentically gay male theology of liberation. In closing, I want to recall some of the principles I have raised. They may be able to guide us in our attempts to answer the questions I have left untouched, as well as the ones that will surprise us in times to come.

Above all, our theology must arise from and contribute to history. This principle is true of any liberation theology, since liberation is, after all, an event in history; it sets our theology against much that is traditional in Christian theology. Carter Heyward has shown why. She sees that the dead end at which the traditional theologies have arrived began with the definitions of Christ handed down at Chalcedon, part of the compromise Christianity made to become a state religion:

> History became a waiting room for some other world. . . . This early doctrinal development signalled a critical shift in the understanding of how justice is established and by whom: a shift from work in history to faith in that which lies beyond history; a shift from *humanity's* responsibility for creating justice to *God's* gift of a 'natural' justice; a shift from the love of one's neighbor in the world to the love of one's God above the world.[1]

Love is the grounds of our oppression, for our love is, in the words of the teaching church speaking on behalf of society's prejudice, disordered. Love, then, must be the ground on which our theology is built.

But this requires us to be clear and careful about what we mean by love. Heyward's definition of love as justice is central to any gay male liberation theology, though it is a standard that applies to everyone. We can each test our own loves against it by asking whether they are consistent with solidarity. The Brazilian bishop Pedro Casaldáliga teaches us why: "Solidarity," he writes, "must be considered not a right but a duty. Solidarity is love made public, collective and political."[2] In it, love must be a dimension of history, not just a human attraction, still less an attribute of God alone.

Our Own Two Feet: Love and History

How we will look at love will depend on what we believe about human beings. This is the theological dimension of reclaiming our self-definition from "experts." Because our bodies and what we do with them are what our oppressors hate, our bodies are where we must begin. If Chalcedonian Christianity took away our access to historical action, it left the door open to respect for our bodies. It was at Chalcedon that the church affirmed the unity of Christ's human and divine natures (Heyward has noted that it did so at the expense of the voluntary quality of God's becoming flesh—but the godliness of the flesh is still admitted). This is a place where we can boast of our continuity with the oldest Christian traditions.

Latin theologians, under the spell of Augustine's argument with Pelagius, have been reluctant to take the incarnation to its logical conclusion. Augustinian theology is where we get our ideas of original sin, the taint we all are supposed to inherit from Adam. Byzantine theologians worried less about original sin. Gay men can take heart from what John of Damascus (like Augustine, a Doctor of the Church) teaches about our humanity:

> God created [human beings] innocent, straightforward, virtuous, free from pain, free from care, ornamented with every virtue, and adorned with all good qualities. [God] made [us] a sort of miniature world within the larger one . . . earthly and heavenly, passing and immortal, visible and spiritual, halfway between greatness and lowliness, at once spirit and flesh. . . . [God] moreover made [us] sinless and endowed with freedom of will. By being sinless I do not mean being incapable of sinning, for only the Divinity is incapable of sinning, but having the tendency to sin not in [our] nature, but rather, in [our] power of choice.[3]

This view of human nature as essentially good is even more powerfully expressed by Maximus the Confessor, developing what has come to be called his theology of "deification." Maximus taught that God became a human being in order that human beings might become God. We put on Christ in baptism and thus free the Christ nature in ourselves. Maximus also drew from the oneness of God the understanding that love, too, is one: God is eros and agape both and, at the same time, the object of each. As eros, God is moved; as agape, God moves.

There is a problem of method we must deal with before we can fully reclaim this tradition. I have alluded to it. Not only have men dominated theology, not only have straight people (at least, people we would now call straight) dominated it, so, too, people vowed to celibacy have dominated it, at least in the Roman, Eastern, and, to a certain extent, Anglican traditions. Working from their own lives, as is proper, but claiming to represent universal principles, they planted in our theological thinking a habit of treating sexual affection as part of our "fallenness." It is long past time to question this premise. Not only gay men but the whole church will benefit.

I say this because we must keep in mind that a gay male liberation theology is not just for us. It is a gift to the whole church. Sheila Rowbotham's reminder that "we are going to have to take them with us" is not just self-protection. It is inseparable from the outward spiral I describe in this book. It is solidarity.

Liturgy, the Work of the People

We must begin from our bodies and our lives. But our oppressors have been preaching that how we use our bodies and how we live in relation to others is wrong. Our oppression is relational, as our creation was, as our resurrection is, and, therefore, as our liberation will be.

No one, prophet or king, can liberate others. Those are the lessons of Moses' journeys and of Jesus' triumphal entry. But there is no individual salvation. That is the lesson of Esther. It is the nature of politics and it is our nature: in the image of God as male and female together are we made, not alone. This is true of our social relations and it is true of each one of us. Each of us must eat the matzo of slavery and put on Christ in the baptismal waters of the Red Sea and the River Jordan.

We must do our own work of liberation with our own bodies,

and we must also reflect among ourselves about the meaning of that work in our own lives. But we dare not hope to achieve our liberation at others' expense. We have a duty to their liberation as well. That means we must be involved with lesbian liberation theologies, with feminist theologies, with African-American and Latina and Latino and Native American theologies. We must learn from and challenge one another's theological insights, since, as every writer knows, you can never proofread your own work.

If we dare not cut ourselves off from other oppressed Christians, neither may we cut ourselves off from our gay brothers who are not Christians. They have too much to teach us. This is true especially of those who once were Christians. The fact that they were angry enough to leave the church is a mark of deep love, because only the indifferent do not care enough to leave. It is also true of those who have not been formed by the antisex and antigay pressures of our Christian culture. What it means to love other men in a Buddhist culture or one grounded in the veneration of creation can teach us much—if we have the humility to learn—about how God hopes we will live as gay men in this culture.

We can also learn the rituals these non-Christian brothers use to celebrate our common gay lives. I have already proposed that we should look to the liturgy as an important vehicle for doing theology as gay men. There are two reasons for this. First, we are not allowed to forget our bodies as long as we are engaged in liturgy. Second, liturgical work is where we are most distinctively present to the whole church already. It is where we have always brought some of our gifts. It is where we can start bringing other gifts too.

In the liturgy, we break the Word and we break bread, but breaking is not why we come. We perform these ritual acts to recreate the body of Christ and to become one people of God around the table. Just so, gay men are not creating our theology to break the body of Christ. We break the Word of God open so that we can see into its depths. We break bread together to be united to one another. We will raise our voices in song and in prayer, just as we always have; what will be different is that we will use our real voices and call out our own names. The body is damaged not when our presence around the table is acknowledged but when it is forbidden, when a piece of the body is cut off and thrown away. We do not want to be sent off to a separate table in the parlor, like younger cousins at a family Thanksgiving; but by denying that we are capable of speaking for ourselves, by forbidding us to behave like Christians, even to make mistakes like other Christians, the churches turn us into infants.

"Infants" comes from a Latin word that means "not speaking." We can prove that we are not infants only by speaking up, loud and clear. What gay men say may be new and shocking. So was what Jesus said, and what he did was more shocking still. We put on Jesus in baptism; small wonder if what follows is shocking. But by putting on Christ in baptism, by eating and drinking at Christ's table, we not only take on the Christ nature but undertake to carry on the Christ work: one bread, one body.

One bread, one body: this is the mark of the whole church, as it is the mark of any true part of it. The work we do in particular is at the same time the work of all. Martin Duberman is a gay man who has made many contibutions, as historian, playwright, and activist, both to our people and to the whole society. He can speak from long experience about this paradox. He writes:

> Reclaiming the history of gender nonconformity—which some argue is conterminous if not wholly synonymous with the history of "gays" and "lesbians"—is also a way of confirming another truth of value to *all* human beings, regardless of their sexual orientation. And that is the demonstrable ability of people who are "different" to develop, in the face of denunciation and oppression, creative strategies for survival that then open up new possibilities for everyone. We are all far more different (though not necessarily in sexual ways) than most of us would care to admit in our conformist culture. The emerging history of lesbians and gay men has begun to provide empowering evidence for *anyone* insistent on allowing their differentness to emerge—and on it being respected.[4]

I would add a particular example of this: men in our culture have been kept from learning to care for one another. Homophobia is how this is done; heterosexism is the structure built from this ban. To the extent that gay men have been forced to unlearn homophobia in order to love one another, we can help all men do so.

This will not benefit men only. Women have been forced to do our work of caring for us. Lesbians have been quick to point out to me and my gay brothers our habit of relying on them for community instead of doing the harder work of becoming friends with our lovers. They have been right to refuse any longer to listen to us whine about other gay men's shallowness. Men's learning to care for one another will remove an obstacle in women's road toward liberation.

Furthermore, this ban on men caring for one another was

necessary to the development of capitalism at its most exploitative. If care is segregated in the bourgeois family and women are expected to give themselves up to provide it, men are free to use the public sphere (which is reserved to them) to exploit others. Latin American liberation theologians have explained poverty in their countries by pointing to the system of development that benefits U.S. and European capital by exploiting Latin American labor and raw materials. Dismantling heterosexism, the structure that permits men to exploit others with a good conscience, will help undermine the domination of the north over the south.

Another benefit flows from this. Militarism and war are, in modern times, tools of capital. Homophobia, because it is a sanction against straying from traditional norms of masculinity, including the one that links masculinity with a willingness to use violence, has helped capital co-opt men into sacrificing their bodies and lives for its benefit, even when they do not share that benefit.

In these ways, gay male liberation is our part of the whole revolutionary project of our time.[5]

Love, the Spark of Revolution

How are we to achieve this revolutionary change? Gay men share with other revolutionaries the need to construct a system of ethical norms that will allow our revolution to grow in a seedbed of justice. For Christian gay men, this must be consistent with Christian ethics, but it will have its own answers for the questions that affect us particularly: new answers, perhaps, since the questions are necessarily new.

This, too, is a joint task. My own experience is too narrow for me to dare offer general rules. (I have dared too much already!) I do want to offer a caution, however, based on what I have experienced in circles of gay male Christians as we have wrestled with this problem.

The norm of Christian life is not "do what feels good as long as it doesn't hurt anyone else." The reason has nothing to do with permissiveness or moral relativism. It certainly has nothing to do with any opposition to pleasure. Such a norm is simply too banal for a people who have been incorporated into God's body by baptism in the waters of death and life. It cannot restore the image of God in us.

Nor does it do us any good to pretend there is no sin or that we bear no individual responsibility for it. John of Damascus, for all his praise of human nature, did not deny the human capacity for sin. What we gay men need is to free ourselves from the falsehood that gayness is the root of our sins and learn to make it instead the source of our virtues. Who can model better than we the joy—the gaiety—of Jesus' loving community?

Accustomed to nothing, we have settled for much less than God wants for us. Remember the story of the woman who anointed Jesus' feet: our forgiveness is in proportion to the vastness of our love. I will tell one last story to illustrate this. It offers us a vision in words uniquely our own.

One of the bits of slang that make up gay men's language is the phrase "flaming queen." Sometimes it is reduced, in keeping with the genius of the English language, to the single word "flamer." It is not necessarily a term of approval, referring as it does to someone who is very obviously gay. Its usual antonyms, significantly enough, are "discreet" and "straight-acting."

The latter terms have come to be used among gay men as compliments. The vanguard of the Stonewall Rebellion, though, were flamers. It is time to reclaim them as part of our Christian heritage. The flamers of Stonewall show us what we can accomplish when we are fairies down to the feet.

Their example is profoundly Christian. A story retold by Thomas Merton crystallizes what I have been trying to say throughout this book. It refers to the contemplative life rather than the active life we have been struggling with together, but the question posed in it is the same one I asked as I began: "What must I do to be saved?" The answer has helped me more than once to keep struggling.

> Abbot Lot came to Abbot Joseph and said: Father, according as I am able, I keep my little rule, and my fast, my prayer, meditation and contemplative silence; and according as I am able I strive to cleanse my heart of thoughts: now what more should I do? The elder rose up in reply and stretched out his hands to heaven, and his fingers became like ten lamps of fire. He said: Why not be totally changed into fire?[6]

Why not indeed? It is an aim worthy of Stonewall and of all our martyrs.

What more is there, then, except to gather with all the holy lovers of our history and of our lives, around God's altar or around the coffee table of an AIDS hospice, and join in a great prayer of thanksgiving?[7]

ONE: Lift up your hearts.

ALL: We keep them with God.

ONE: Let us give God thanks and praise.

ALL: It is fitting and just.

ONE: It is fitting and it is just, O God of love, to give you thanks, always and everywhere, for knitting our hearts and bodies into one heart, one body of Christ. As you came among us embodied in human flesh, touching and being touched, healing broken bodies by laying on your hands, and eating with outcasts to restore them to your loving circle of friends,

   So we, gathered here today in friendship and love,
   Join our voices with all those past and present
      and yet to come,
   Singing, shouting, rejoicing in the angels' hymn of praise:

ALL: Holy, holy, holy is the sovereign God of power and might.
   Heaven and earth are full of your glory:
      Hosanna in the highest.
   Blessed is the One who comes in the name of God most high:
      Hosanna in the highest.

ONE: Before the beginning of time,
      the power of your love was so great
         your Unity could not contain it,
   so we praise it instead in the mystery of your Trinity.

   At time's beginning the energy of your love
      poured itself out in the wonder of creation.
   For five days you labored and built,
      and on the sixth you created us in the image of your love,
         not as one being but as two,
         so that we should not be alone.

   When first we fell into selfishness and strife,
      you washed away our wickedness in the Flood,
         restoring every species, two by two.

   We fell into slavery because we no longer knew who we were;
      but you brought us out into freedom,
         leading us through the waters of confusion and death
            into new life together.

At the mountain of your covenant, you called us
   to bind ourselves in love
      to you and to each other
         and to make ourselves a new people.

Time after time we fell from love,
   worshiping wealth and beating down the poor,
      seeking to control others by fear,
      and in fear seeking to protect ourselves from others.

Time and again you raised up outcasts,
   foreigners, and lawbreakers,
      lovers of you and lovers of each other,
      to lead us back into harmony:

ALL: Shiphrah and Puah, the Hebrew midwives,
Jethro the priest of Midian,
   and Rahab the harlot of Jericho
Gideon the fearful, Samson the sensual,
   Deborah the unwomanly,
Naomi the widow without sons
   and Ruth the immigrant field-worker,
David the fugitive and Jonathan the supplanted,
Elijah and Esther, Hosea and Gomer and Job.

ONE: In the fullness of time, as we suffered under new oppressors,
      seeking refuge and meaning not in each other
         but in patterns of habit and rule,
you took on our flesh,
      conceived out of wedlock and born of a strong maid.

You walked our dusty roads,
   offering us signs of healing,
      stories of hope and love.
Still sunk in fear we demanded proof of your love,
   and to give it you gave yourself
      to suffering and death,
so that on the third day you might rise again
   and show yourself alive in the midst of your friends.

ALL: And we knew you in the breaking of the bread.

ONE: For on the night you were abandoned and betrayed
      by those who loved you,
you took the unleavened bread of the Passover,
      said the blessing, and broke it,

and shared it among them all, saying:
    "Take, eat: this is my body,
    broken and offered for love of you."

In the same way you took the cup of blessing and celebration,
    gave thanks for it and said:
    "Take, drink of this, all of you:
    this is the cup of my blood
    poured out to show my love for you.
    When you do this again, do it remembering me."

Faithful to that memory, we join in proclaiming
    the ground of our faith:

ALL: We eat and drink in mutual love,
    joined in remembrance that you died for love of us.

ONE: Remembering indeed your death for love of us,
    we remember too that your love makes us one body,
      members each of one another.

Therefore we remember also those not here among us now,
    those we love who are scattered across the earth,
      and we call them into our midst through memory
        and by lifting up their names.

These and all we love
    we remember and lift up as though they were here,
      in communion with the saints.

ALL: With Martha and Mary and Lazarus,
    with Perpetua and Felicity, with Sergius and Bacchus,
    with Achilleus and Nereus, Paula and Eustochium,
    with Bernard and Malachy, Edmund and Richard,
    with Aelred the Abbot, Joan the Maid, and Angela the Teacher,
    and with those whose names and lives
      have been stolen from all knowledge and all telling.

ONE: Joining our voices with these and all your saints, we pray:

ALL: Most Holy Trinity,
    send down your Spirit, the presence of your love,
    to make these gifts holy, and to make us holy with them,
      to make us one in you and in love of one another.

ONE: Finally,
    remembering how your love led you
      to the shameful death of a criminal on a cross;

remembering too how those
who walked in love with you in the flesh
came also to die in disgrace;
remembering too how our mothers and fathers in the faith
held themselves ready to die for love of you;
remembering too how today we risk death and violence
at the hands of those who hate us for our love;
we call to mind those who have fallen asleep in your love,
by hatred,
violence,
accident,
disease,
or the merciful passing of time,
and who now are waiting to greet us
on the shore of the river we too one day must cross,
especially those whose names we now offer.

By human labor, once,
seeds of grain were scattered on the earth.
They died and sprouted, bore fruit and were gathered,
and were made by human labor
into the bread and wine that now we share in love.

We give thanks for the labor of others' hands
for the witness of their lives,
and the gifts of their love,
and pray that all your people
may at last in love be gathered
from the four winds and the corners of the world,
to rise as one body of Christ at the end of time.

And so, together in love with all here present,
with those we love across the world,
with those who have gone before,
and those who are yet to come into our lives,
we offer to the loving God of all
this sacrifice of thanks and praise,
and to one another, a holy kiss.

ALL: Amen!

Notes

Preface

1. Barbara Ehrenreich, *Fear of Falling: The Inner Life of the Middle Class* (New York: Pantheon Books, 1989), 5.
2. [Isabel] Carter Heyward, *The Redemption of God: A Theology of Mutual Relation* (Lanham, Md.: University Press of America, 1982), 30.

Introduction: Announcing the Jubilee

1. Michael Goodich, *The Unmentionable Vice: Homosexuality in the Later Medieval Period* (Santa Barbara, Calif.: Ross-Erikson, 1979), 9. Goodich gives examples of the association between sodomy and heresy, as well as noting the elements of class conflict in antisodomy campaigns and their further association with attacks on Judaism and Islam.
2. Reported by John Zeitler, personal communication with author, March 2, 1988.
3. Leonardo Boff, *The Maternal Face of God: The Feminine and Its Religious Expressions,* trans. Robert R. Barr and John W. Diercksmeier (San Francisco: Harper & Row, 1987), 10.
4. Gustavo Gutiérrez, *A Theology of Liberation: History, Politics and Salvation,* trans. Caridad Inda and John Eagleson (Maryknoll, N.Y.: Orbis Books, 1973), 6.
5. Ibid., 7.
6. Juan Luis Segundo, *The Liberation of Theology,* trans. John Drury (Maryknoll, N.Y.: Orbis Books, 1976), 8.
7. Ibid., 8–9.
8. Dorothee Soelle, *The Strength of the Weak: Toward a Christian Feminist Identity* (Philadelphia: Westminster, 1984), 90.
9. Paul Tillich, *Systematic Theology* (Chicago: University of Chicago Press, 1963), 1:10.
10. Paraphrased from remarks by Harvey Cox in a broadcast lecture at the University of Michigan in Ann Arbor in the mid-1980s.
11. George R. Edwards, *Gay/Lesbian Liberation: A Biblical Perspective* (New York: Pilgrim, 1984), title of chap. 5.

Chapter 1: God Makes a New People

1. An excellent summary and discussion of the current state of historical thinking can be found in Martin Duberman's 1991 talks at the Museum of Natural History in New York, published in the revised edition of his *About Time: Exploring the Gay Past* (New York: Meridian, 1991), 436–67.
2. Lillian Faderman, *Odd Girls and Twilight Lovers* (New York: Columbia University Press, 1991), chap. 7, 159–87; and George Chauncey, *Gay New York* (New York: Basic Books, 1994), passim.
3. Manfred Herzer, "Kertbeny and the Nameless Love," *Journal of Homosexuality* 12, 1 (1986):1–26.
4. Lawrence R. Murphy, *Perverts by Official Order: The Campaign against Homosexuals by the United States Navy* (New York: Harrington Park, 1988). The classic surveys of U.S. lesbian and gay male history from which I have drawn most of my material for this section are: John D'Emilio, *Sexual Politics, Sexual Communities: The Making of a Homosexual Minority in the United States* (Chicago: University of Chicago Press, 1983); Lillian Faderman, *Odd Girls and Twilight Lovers: A History of Lesbian Life in Twentieth-Century America* (New York: Columbia University Press, 1991); and two documentary collections by Jonathan Katz, *Gay American History: Lesbians and Gay Men in the U.S.A.* (New York: Avon Discus, 1978), and *Gay/Lesbian Almanac: A New Documentary* (New York: Harper & Row, 1983).
4. John Lauritsen and David Thorstad, *The Early Homosexual Rights Movement (1864–1935)* (New York: Times Change, 1974), 60.
5. The German movement is described by John Lauritsen and David Thorstad, *The Early Homosexual Rights Movement (1864–1935)* (New York: Times Change, 1974).
6. Marvin Cutler, *Homosexuals Today* (Los Angeles: ONE, Inc., 1956), 93.
7. I believe the real long-term significance of John Boswell's well-known and controversial *Christianity, Social Tolerance and Homosexuality: Gay People in Western Europe from the Beginning of the Christian Era to the Fourteenth Century* (Chicago: University of Chicago Press, 1980) is that it demolishes the church's grounds for claiming that tradition has always and everywhere taught the same thing on these matters. This is an important test of theological truth in traditional Catholic theology, one the magisterium has now been shown to have failed.
8. Martin Luther King, Jr., *Letter from a Birmingham Jail* (New York: A. J. Muste Memorial Institute, n.d.), 29–30.
9. Claude J. Summers, "Book Review: Byron and Greek Love," *Journal of Homosexuality* 15, 3/4 (1988): 143–55.

Chapter 2: Naming and Power

1. This controversy is described in Shira Maguen, "Teen Suicide: The Government's Cover-up and America's Lost Children," in *A Certain*

Terror: Heterosexism, Militarism, Violence and Change, ed. Richard Cleaver and Patricia Myers (Chicago: Great Lakes Region, American Friends Service Committee, 1993), 239–49.

2. George Chauncey, *Gay New York: Gender, Urban Culture, and the Making of the Gay Male World, 1890–1940* (New York: Basic Books, 1994), 7–8.
3. Hubert Kennedy, *Ulrichs: The Life and Works of Karl Heinrich Ulrichs, Pioneer of the Modern Gay Movement* (Boston: Alyson Publications, 1988), 176.
4. The phrase "intrinsically disordered" is used in the Sacred Congregation for the Doctrine of the Faith's "Declaration on Certain Questions Concerning Sexual Ethics" of December 19, 1975, found in *Homosexuality and the Magisterium: Documents from the Vatican and U.S. Bishops, 1975–1985,* ed. John Gallagher (Mt. Rainier, Md.: New Ways Ministry, 1986).
5. Antony Grey, "The Church's Role after Law Reform," in *Is Gay Good? Ethics, Theology and Homosexuality,* ed. W. Dwight Oberholtzer (Philadelphia: Westminster, 1971), 199.
6. Heyward, *Redemption of God,* 17.
7. John Boswell, *Same-Sex Unions in Premodern Europe* (New York: Villard Books, 1994), 5–9.
8. I have been unable to track down where I came across Maximus the Confessor's insightful commentary on the two words. He follows pseudo-Denis in teaching that God is both eros and agape and, at the same time, the object of each. As the first, Maximus tells us, God is moved; as the second, God moves.
9. Chauncey, *Gay New York,* 72–76.
10. Louis Crompton, *Byron and Greek Love: Homophobia in 19th-Century England* (Berkeley and Los Angeles: University of California Press, 1985), 56. On the subject of xenophobia: Boswell (*Same-Sex Unions,* 365) quotes the medieval rabbi Nachmanides as teaching that the Sodomites acted as they did "to stop people from coming among them, as our Rabbis have said, for they thought that because of the excellence of their land, which was *as the garden of the Eternal* [emphasis in Boswell], many will come there. . . ." This is remarkably, and ironically, similar to one of the arguments occasionally used against including lesbians and gay men in local civil rights ordinances: doing so, some claim, will lure more of us to the town in question.
11. Richard Hofstadter, *The Paranoid Style in American Politics and Other Essays* (New York: Alfred A. Knopf, 1965), 21.
12. Monika K. Hellwig, *Theology as Fine Art* (Wilmington: Michael Glazier, 1983), 10.
13. Sheila Rowbotham, *Woman's Consciousness, Man's World* (Harmondsworth: Penguin Books, 1973), xiii.
14. Ibid., xii.
15. Gary Kinsman, *The Regulation of Desire: Sexuality in Canada* (Montreal: Black Rose Books, 1987), 91.

16. This is one of the major theses of Allan Bérubé's book *Coming Out under Fire: The History of Gay Men and Women in World War II* (New York: NAL-Dutton, Plume Books, 1991). Kinsman (*Regulation of Desire,* 110–11) discusses why the same did not happen in Canada. In this context, I should note that I am aware that one of the arguments used by essentialists against social constructionists is that the latter tend to fall into a nominalist trap, believing that the ability to name ourselves as lesbians or gay men is the determining historical event in developing our collective identity. What I have said in this chapter may suggest that I agree; I do not, but there is no good place in this book to engage in that debate directly, important as it is.

Chapter 3: In the Image of God

1. Sally Gearhart, "The Miracle of Lesbianism," in *Loving Women/Loving Men,* ed. Sally Gearhart and William R. Johnson (San Francisco: Glide Publications, 1974), 127. (The pastor of Glide Memorial Church, which published this book, was and still is the Reverend Cecil Williams, an important figure in the Council on Religion and the Homosexual, mentioned in chapter 1 of this book at the end of the section "Makers of History.")
2. Ibid., 135.
3. Ibid., 127–28.
4. I use the NRSV translation of the longer, Greek version of Esther, which is canonical for Roman Catholics and Eastern Orthodox. The two versions are independently rendered and the NRSV prints the Greek version among the Apocrypha; readers who consult only the shorter, Hebrew version will notice some discrepancies in translation.
5. Robert W. Wood, "Rahab, the Harlot of Jericho," *ONE Magazine* 8, no. 12 (December 1960): 6–8.
6. For the history of Nazi persecution of lesbians and gay men, the classic source is Richard Plant, *The Pink Triangle: The Nazi War against Homosexuals* (New York: Henry Holt, 1986). A survivor's personal account in English is Heinz Heger, *The Men with the Pink Triangle* (Boston: Alyson Publications, 1980).
7. Ethan Mordden, *Buddies* (New York: St. Martin's, 1986), 38.
8. Johann Baptist Metz, *The Emergent Church,* trans. Peter Mann (New York: Crossroad, 1981), 6.
9. Ibid., 6–7.
10. This is not the place for a detailed critique of Midge Decter's *Commentary* article; I have written elsewhere about Decter and Podhoretz's writing and its historical context. See Richard Cleaver, "Sexual Dissidents and the National Security State, 1942–1992," in Cleaver and Myers, *A Certain Terror* (Chicago: Great Lakes Region, American Friends Service Committee, 1993), 202–5.

11. Soelle, *Strength of the Weak,* 32.
12. Ibid., 40.
13. Heyward, *Redemption of God,* 2.

Chapter 4: What God Has Made Clean

1. The vindicta was a ritual rod used in the emancipation of a Roman slave. See Kennedy, *Ulrichs,* 68.
2. *The Sunday Missal,* ed. Harold Winstone (London: Collins Liturgical Publications, 1977), 211.
3. Crompton, *Byron and Greek Love,* 234–35.
4. Historian Martin Duberman makes just this point throughout his book on the subject, *Stonewall* (New York: Plume, 1994).
5. This is discussed in chapter 7 of Toby Marotta, *The Politics of Homosexuality* (Boston: Houghton Mifflin, 1981).
6. Quoted in Kay Tobin and Randy Wicker, *The Gay Crusaders* (New York: Arno, 1975), 197.
7. See Barbara Ehrenreich's examination of this tendency in *Fear of Falling: The Inner Life of the Middle Class* (New York: Pantheon Books, 1989).
8. E. P. Thompson, *The Making of the English Working Class* (New York: Pantheon Books, 1964), 9.
9. Ibid., 11.
10. Ibid.
11. Ibid., 9.
12. Ibid., 10.
13. Ibid., 11.
14. To understand the historical similarities and differences, see Harlan Lane's account of the growth and subsequent near destruction of a vibrant and conscious nineteenth-century Deaf culture in *When the Mind Hears* (New York: Random House, 1984). Two points are in order about the terminology I have used in the text and in the opening part of this note. First, the phrase "disability groups" is coming to be used among disabled activists to refer to the various diagnostic categories within the larger world of people with disabilities: blindness, spinal cord injury, multiple sclerosis, deafness, and so on. Second, the capitalized form "Deaf" is used when referring to people who identify with Deaf culture, as opposed to people with the physiological condition of hearing loss, for whom the lowercase form is used. A good resource for keeping abreast of these issues is a periodical, *The Disability Rag.*
15. In David Thorstad, ed., *Gay Liberation and Socialism: Documents from the Discussions on Gay Liberation inside the Socialist Workers Party (1970–1973)* (New York: privately printed, 1976), 57.
16. Ibid.
17. Metz, *Emergent Church,* 6.

18. Ibid., 4.
19. Soelle, *Strength of the Weak,* 39.
20. Ibid., 45.
21. See Metz, *Emergent Church,* 83.
22. William Dean Howells, *The Quality of Mercy* (New York: Harper & Brothers, 1892), 14.
23. Karl Marx and Friedrich Engels, *The German Ideology,* Parts I and III, trans. R. Pascal (New York: International Publishers, 1947), 40.
24. Virgil Elizondo, *The Future Is Mestizo: Life Where Cultures Meet* (Bloomington, Ind.: Meyer-Stone Books, 1988), 77.
25. Ibid., 78.
26. Ibid., 80.

Chapter 5: In the Breaking of the Bread

1. See Rowbotham, *Woman's Consciousness, Man's World,* 41.
2. Ibid., 38.
3. Ibid., 36.
4. George Chauncey, *Gay New York: Gender, Urban Culture, and the Making of the Gay Male World, 1890–1940* (New York: Basic Books, 1994), chap. 8, 206–25.
5. The controversy is discussed by the biographer, Blanche Wiesen Cook, in "Outing History II: Eleanor—Loves of a First Lady," *The Nation,* 5 July 1993, 24, 26. She broadens her discussion in "Outing History," *Out,* no. 10 (February–March 1994): 50, 52–54.
6. Douglass Roby, introduction to Aelred of Rievaulx, *Spiritual Friendship,* trans. Mary Eugenia Laker (Kalamazoo, Mich.: Cistercian Publications, 1977), 21–22.
7. Martin Duberman, "Hidden from History," in *About Time,* 442–43.
8. What is this mysterious and otherwise unchronicled appearance? In rereading the story of the raising of Lazarus, I find myself wondering: Could it be that as Peter puzzled over his visit to the tomb, so like the one near Bethany described by John, he suddenly recalled the raising of their friend and so caused Jesus to be present to him again?
9. Lucien Deiss, *Early Sources of the Liturgy,* trans. Benet Weatherhead, 2d ed. (Collegeville, Minn.: Liturgical Press, 1975), 14.
10. Chauncey, *Gay New York,* 293–94.
11. John Boswell, *Rediscovering Gay History* (London: Gay Christian Movement, 1982), 18–21.
12. John Boswell, *Same-Sex Unions in Premodern Europe* (New York: Villard Books, 1994), 5–9. For recent revivals, see the review of this book by Bruce Holsinger in *The Nation* 259, no. 7 (Sept. 5–12, 1994): 241–44.
13. Arthur Evans discusses Joan's career and her ties with the old religion in the first chapter of *Witchcraft and the Gay Counterculture* (Boston: Fag Rag

Books, 1978). He also argues, convincingly, that the tradition of celebrating Halloween by transvestism is a survival of pre-Christian practice.

Chapter 6: One Bread, One Body

1. Heyward, *Redemption of God,* 5.
2. Pedro Casaldáliga, "Letter of December 1988," *Latinamerica Press* 21, no. 1 (January 5, 1989): 60.
3. John of Damascus, *The Orthodox Faith: Book One (The Fount of Knowledge, Part III),* trans. Frederic H. Chase (Washington, D.C.: Catholic University of America Press, 1970), 235.
4. Martin Duberman, "Outing History I: A Matter of Difference," *The Nation,* 5 July 1993, 24.
5. For a more detailed discussion along the same lines but from the point of view of a gay male theologian of the old religion, see chapter 10, "Magic and Revolution," in Evans, *Witchcraft and the Gay Counterculture.*
6. Thomas Merton, *The Wisdom of the Desert: Sayings from the Desert Fathers of the Fourth Century* (New York: New Directions, 1960), 50.
7. The following prayer is offered for liturgical use by anybody. After the passage "Therefore we remember also those not here among us now . . . by lifting up their names," those gathered say aloud the names of living but absent friends and family. Similarly, at the commemoration of the dead, after the line, "especially those whose names we now offer," those present say aloud the names of their beloved dead. The prayer ends, suiting action to words, with a general Kiss of Peace.

Bibliography

Aelred of Rievaulx. *Spiritual Friendship*. Translated by Mary Eugenia Laker. Kalamazoo, Mich.: Cistercian Publications, 1977.

Bérubé, Allan. *Coming Out under Fire: The History of Gay Men and Women in World War II*. New York: NAL-Dutton, Plume Books, 1991.

Boff, Leonardo. *The Maternal Face of God: The Feminine and Its Religious Expressions*. Translated by Robert R. Barr and John W. Diercksmeier. San Francisco: Harper & Row, 1987.

Boswell, John. *Christianity, Social Tolerance and Homosexuality: Gay People in Western Europe from the Beginning of the Christian Era to the Fourteenth Century*. Chicago: University of Chicago Press, 1980.

————. *Rediscovering Gay History*. London: Gay Christian Movement, 1982.

————. *Same-Sex Unions in Premodern Europe*. New York: Villard Books, 1994.

Bray, Alan. *Homosexuality in Renaissance England*. London: Gay Men's Press, 1982.

Bronski, Michael. *Culture Clash: The Making of Gay Sensibility*. Boston: South End, 1984.

Casaldáliga, Pedro. "Letter of December 1988." *Latinamerica Press* 21, no. 1 (January 5, 1989): 60.

Chauncey, George. *Gay New York: Gender, Urban Culture, and the Making of the Gay Male World, 1890–1940*. New York: Basic Books, 1994.

Cleaver, Richard, and Patricia Myers, eds. *A Certain Terror: Heterosexism, Militarism, Violence and Change*. Chicago: Great Lakes Region, American Friends Service Committee, 1993.

————. *New Heaven, New Earth: Practical Essays on the Catholic Worker Program*. Edited by Beth Preheim and Michael Sprong. Marion, S.D.: Rose Hill Books, 1993.

Cone, James H. *A Black Theology of Liberation*. 2d ed. Maryknoll, N.Y.: Orbis Books, 1986.

Cook, Blanche Wiesen. "Outing History II: Eleanor—Loves of a First Lady." *The Nation*, July 5, 1993, 24, 26.

———. "Outing History." *OUT*, no. 10 (February–March 1994): 50, 52–54.

Crompton, Louis. *Byron and Greek Love: Homophobia in 19th-Century England*. Berkeley and Los Angeles: University of California Press, 1985.

Cutler, Marvin. *Homosexuals Today*. Los Angeles: ONE, Inc., 1956.

Decter, Midge. "The Boys on the Beach." *Commentary* (September 1980): 35–48.

Deiss, Lucien. *Early Sources of the Liturgy*. Translated by Benet Weatherhead. 2d ed. Collegeville, Minn.: Liturgical Press, 1975.

D'Emilio, John. *Sexual Politics, Sexual Communities: The Making of a Homosexual Minority in the United States*. Chicago: University of Chicago Press, 1983.

D'Emilio, John, and Estelle B. Freedman. *Intimate Matters: A History of Sexuality in America*. New York: Harper & Row, 1988.

Duberman, Martin. *About Time: Exploring the Gay Past*. Revised and expanded ed. New York: Meridian, 1991.

———. "Outing History I: A Matter of Difference." *The Nation*, July 5, 1993, 22–24.

———. *Stonewall*. New York: Plume, 1994.

Edwards, George R. *Gay/Lesbian Liberation: A Biblical Perspective*. New York: Pilgrim, 1984.

Ehrenreich, Barbara. *Fear of Falling: The Inner Life of the Middle Class*. New York: Pantheon Books, 1989.

Elizondo, Virgil. *The Future Is Mestizo: Life Where Cultures Meet*. Bloomington, Ind.: Meyer-Stone Books, 1988.

Evans, Arthur. *Witchcraft and the Gay Counterculture*. Boston: Fag Rag Books, 1978.

Faderman, Lillian. *Odd Girls and Twilight Lovers: A History of Lesbian Life in Twentieth-Century America*. New York: Columbia University Press, 1991.

Fiorenza, Elisabeth Schüssler. *In Memory of Her: A Feminist Theological Reconstruction of Christian Origins*. New York: Crossroad, 1983.

Gallagher, John, ed. *Homosexuality and the Magisterium: Documents from the Vatican and the U.S. Bishops, 1975–1985*. Mt. Rainier, Md.: New Ways Ministry, 1986.

Gearhart, Sally. "The Miracle of Lesbianism." In *Loving Women/*

Loving Men. Edited by Sally Gearhart and William R. Johnson, 119–52. San Francisco: Glide Publications, 1974.

Goodich, Michael. *The Unmentionable Vice: Homosexuality in the Later Medieval Period.* Santa Barbara, Calif.: Ross-Erikson, 1979.

Grey, Antony. "The Church's Role after Law Reform." In *Is Gay Good? Ethics, Theology and Homosexuality.* Edited by W. Dwight Oberholtzer, 199–203. Philadelphia: Westminster, 1971.

Gutiérrez, Gustavo. *A Theology of Liberation: History, Politics and Salvation.* Translated by Caridad Inda and John Eagleson. Maryknoll, N.Y.: Orbis Books, 1973.

Harrison, Beverly Wildung. *Making the Connections: Essays in Feminist Social Ethics.* Edited by Carol S. Robb. Boston: Beacon, 1985.

Heger, Heinz. *The Men with the Pink Triangle.* Boston: Alyson Publications, 1980.

Hellwig, Monika K. *Theology as a Fine Art.* Wilmington: Michael Glazier, 1983.

Herzer, Manfred. "Kertbeny and the Nameless Love." *Journal of Homosexuality* 12, no. 1 (1986): 1–26.

Heyward, [Isabel] Carter. *The Redemption of God: A Theology of Mutual Relation.* Reprint of dissertation. Lanham, Md.: University Press of America, 1982.

———. *Our Passion for Justice: Images of Power, Sexuality and Liberation.* New York: Pilgrim, 1984.

———. *Speaking of Christ: A Lesbian Feminist Voice.* New York: Pilgrim, 1989.

Hofstadter, Richard. *The Paranoid Style in American Politics and Other Essays.* New York: Alfred A. Knopf, 1965.

Howells, William Dean. *The Quality of Mercy.* New York: Harper & Brothers, 1892.

Isasi-Díaz, Ada María, and Yolanda Tarango. *Hispanic Women: Prophetic Voice in the Church.* San Francisco: Harper & Row, 1988.

John of Damascus. *The Orthodox Faith: Book One (The Fount of Knowledge, Part III).* Translated by Frederic H. Chase. Washington, D.C.: Catholic University of America Press, 1970.

Katz, Jonathan. *Gay American History: Lesbians and Gay Men in the U.S.A.* New York: Avon Discus, 1978.

———. *Gay/Lesbian Almanac: A New Documentary.* New York: Harper & Row, 1983.

Kennedy, Hubert. *Ulrichs: The Life and Works of Karl Heinrich Ulrichs, Pioneer of the Modern Gay Movement.* Boston: Alyson Publications, 1988.

King, Martin Luther, Jr. *Letter from a Birmingham Jail*. Reprint ed. New York: A. J. Muste Memorial Institute, n.d.

Kinsman, Gary. *The Regulation of Desire: Sexuality in Canada*. Montreal: Black Rose Books, 1987.

Lane, Harlan. *When the Mind Hears*. New York: Random House, 1984.

Lauritsen, John, and David Thorstad. *The Early Homosexual Rights Movement (1864–1935)*. New York: Times Change, 1974.

McNeill, John J. *The Church and the Homosexual*. Kansas City, Mo.: Sheed, Andrews & McMeel, 1976.

Maguen, Shira. "Teen Suicide: The Government's Cover-up and America's Lost Children." In *A Certain Terror: Heterosexism, Militarism, Violence and Change*. Edited by Richard Cleaver and Patricia Myers, 239–49. Chicago: Great Lakes Region, American Friends Service Committee, 1993.

Marotta, Toby. *The Politics of Homosexuality*. Boston: Houghton Mifflin, 1981.

Marx, Karl, and Friedrich Engels. *The German Ideology,* Parts I and III. Translated by R. Pascal. New York: International Publishers, 1947.

Ménard, Guy. *De Sodome à l'exode: Jalons pour une théologie de la libération gaie*. Quebec: Guy Saint-Jean, 1982.

Merton, Thomas. *The Wisdom of the Desert: Sayings from the Desert Fathers of the Fourth Century*. New York: New Directions, 1960.

Metz, Johann Baptist. *The Emergent Church*. Translated by Peter Mann. New York: Crossroad, 1981.

Mordden, Ethan. *Buddies*. New York: St. Martin's, 1986.

Murphy, Lawrence R. *Perverts by Official Order: The Campaign against Homosexuals by the United States Navy*. New York: Harrington Park, 1988.

Plant, Richard. *The Pink Triangle: The Nazi War against Homosexuals*. New York: Henry Holt, 1986.

Rowbotham, Sheila. *Woman's Consciousness, Man's World*. Harmondsworth: Penguin Books, 1973.

Ruether, Rosemary Radford. *Faith and Fratricide: The Theological Roots of Anti-Semitism*. New York: Seabury, 1974.

———. *Sexism and God-Talk: Toward a Feminist Theology*. Boston: Beacon, 1983.

Scanzoni, Letha, and Virginia Mollenkott. *Is the Homosexual My Neighbor? Another Christian View*. San Francisco: Harper & Row, 1978.

Segundo, Juan Luis. *The Liberation of Theology.* Translated by John Drury. Maryknoll, N.Y.: Orbis Books, 1976.

Soelle, Dorothee. *The Strength of the Weak: Toward a Christian Feminist Identity.* Philadelphia: Westminster, 1984.

Summers, Claude J. "Book Review: Byron and Greek Love." *Journal of Homosexuality* 15, no. 3/4 (1988): 143–55.

Thompson, E. P. *The Making of the English Working Class.* New York: Pantheon Books, 1964.

Thorstad, David, ed. *Gay Liberation and Socialism: Documents from the Discussions on Gay Liberation inside the Socialist Workers Party (1970–1973).* New York: privately printed, 1976.

Tillich, Paul. *Systematic Theology.* Volume 1. Chicago: University of Chicago Press, 1963.

Tobin, Kay, and Randy Wicker. *The Gay Crusaders.* Reprint ed. New York: Arno, 1975.

Towards a Quaker View of Sex: An Essay by a Group of Friends. Revised ed. London: Friends Home Service Committee, 1964.

Troester, Rosalie Riegle. *Voices from the Catholic Worker.* Philadelphia: Temple University Press, 1993.

Weeks, Jeffrey. *Coming Out: Homosexual Politics in Britain, from the Nineteenth Century to the Present.* London: Quartet Books, 1977.

Wood, Robert W. "Rahab, the Harlot of Jericho." *ONE Magazine* 8, no. 12 (December 1960): 6–8.

Zeitler, John. Personal communication. March 2, 1988.